THE

MYSTERIES

OF INTERNET RESEARCH

SHARRON COHEN

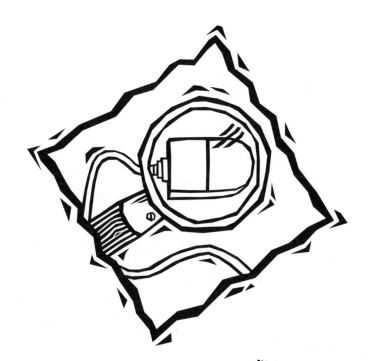

UpstartBooks™

Fort Atkinson, Wisconsin

*To David, Nathan and Jennifer, who cheerfully endured
my daily recitation of fascinating facts.*

Published by UpstartBooks
W5527 Highway 106
P.O. Box 800
Fort Atkinson, Wisconsin 53538-0800
1-800-448-4887

© Sharron Cohen, 2003
Cover design: Debra Neu Sletten

The paper used in this publication meets the minimum requirements of American National Standard for Information Science — Permanence of Paper for Printed Library Material. ANSI/NISO Z39.48-1992.

Contents

To the Librarian or Teacher

The ability to find information is only one of many research skills. The ability to recognize what information needs to be found and the ability to use all the information gained to come to a conclusion about a situation are equally important skills. *The Mysteries of Internet Research* is designed to combine all three aspects of research by giving students a set of problems whose solutions require both logical thought and a search for facts.

A sample exercise, "The Mystery of the Footloose Fleas," is included in the introduction of this book. Working through the sample with your class, you can show students how to decide what to look up, how to research the necessary facts and how to use the clues to reach a logical conclusion.

Levels of Difficulty

The mysteries in this book are divided into three levels of difficulty: Easy, Intermediate and Difficult.

Easy Mysteries

All information needed to solve Easy Mysteries can be found on the following Web sites:

- **Fact Monster.** www.factmonster.com/encyclopedia.html

- **Information Please.** www.infoplease.com

- **Merriam-Webster On-line.** www.m-w.com

- **Mapquest.** www.mapquest.com

- **Biography.com.** www.biography.com

Intermediate Mysteries

Intermediate Mysteries require students to do a broader search. While the sites used in the Easy Mysteries will still be useful, students have to find information on a wider variety of Web sites, and they have to decide for themselves what those Web sites will be. Intermediate Mysteries also contain more information to research and are more difficult to solve. The following search engines are useful:

- **iTools.** www.itools.com

- **Google.** www.google.com

Difficult Mysteries

Difficult Mysteries require students to do more difficult searches and to review longer, more complicated material. Some of the mysteries contain themes, such as murder and drug use, which make them less appropriate for younger students. While innocent suspects still tell the truth, guilty ones weave a combination of truths, lies and misleading facts into their statements. The most challenging mysteries in this category require an extra bit of initiative and intuition from the student.

In addition to the resources used at the Easy and Intermediate levels, one more Web site is useful at the Difficult Mystery level:

- **Babel Fish Translator.** babelfish.altavista.com

At the time of this book's publication, none of the sites mentioned required membership fees or registration.

Increasing/Decreasing Difficulty Levels

Even within the Easy, Intermediate and Difficult Mystery levels, some mysteries are harder than others. The Table of Contents lists them in roughly ascending order of difficulty.

There are several other ways in which the mysteries can be adjusted to the ability levels of your students:

- Deciding what to look up is sometimes as difficult for students as doing the research itself. If that is the case, you can underline some or all of the facts to be researched on the students' copies of the mysteries before they start.

- The first paragraph of each suspect profile, which gives the location of birth and a clue for finding the suspect's age, reveals the guilt or innocence of that suspect. The mysteries can be made more difficult by asking students not to research those two clues until they have researched the body of the suspect profile. They can then use the birth date and birthplace clues to confirm their findings of guilt or innocence.

- In anticipation of problems like vanishing Web sites, and to make the mysteries solvable with print as well as Internet resources, the profile of each suspect contains redundancies—multiple instances of correct or incorrect facts. Students can be required to check every fact or only enough facts to ascertain guilt or innocence. Whichever course is taken, students should be cautioned that failure to find a fact does not prove a suspect's guilt.

- A sample Detective's Report is included on page 21. It can be expanded to require students to write more detailed descriptions of what they find, or students can report their findings to you verbally.

Privacy and Maintenance Concerns

Teaching students how to navigate the Internet safely, without divulging information about themselves and without being distracted by the advertising that floods the Web, is beyond the purview of this book, but it is always a concern. So is the proper maintenance of computers. Someone should be emptying recycle bins, clearing cookies and performing scandisk and defrag functions on computers that come in contact with the World Wide Web.

The following Web sites address these concerns:

- **Privacy Toolbox.**
  www.privacytoolbox.org
  Run by the Internet Education Foundation, Privacy Toolbox offers a general discussion about children's privacy and the Internet.

- **Computer Maintenance Tutorial.**
  www.uwrf.edu/ccs/training/maintain.htm
  Run by the University of Wisconsin–River Falls, this tutorial gives detailed instructions for regular computer maintenance.

Research Detective's
Starter Kit

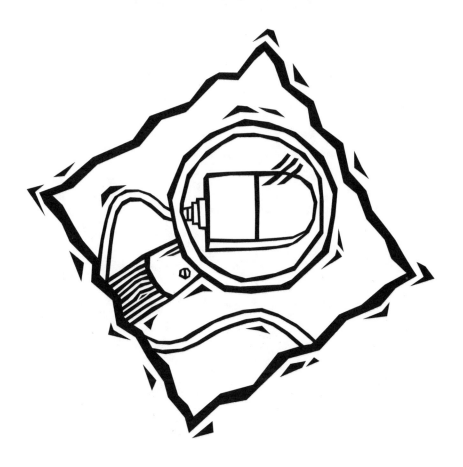

Memorandum to Research Recruits

To: Research Bureau Detective Recruits

From: Research Bureau Chief

Re: An Introduction to the Bureau

Welcome to the Research Bureau. As detective recruits, you are part of an elite corps dedicated to truth, justice and clear thinking.

Very soon, you will be assigned your first case. It will consist of a description of a crime and profiles of four suspects. One or more of the suspects will give erroneous information about themselves. The suspect or suspects who lie are guilty of the crime. It is up to you to bring them to justice by uncovering evidence against them. Using the Internet and your own keen sense of logic, you will determine the following facts:

- which suspects are telling the truth

- which suspect or suspects are lying and are, therefore, guilty

- how the crime was committed

- why the crime was committed

- if something was stolen, where it can be found

To assist you in your endeavors, Detective Ace Primo, the Research Bureau's best detective, has agreed to share her personal notebook with you. Please review its contents before starting work on your case.

Good luck to each of you.

Attachments:
- Detective Primo's Notebook

- Internet Navigation Manual

- Print Resources Navigation Manual

- Internet Navigation at a Glance

- Print Resources at a Glance

Detective Ace Primo's Notebook

Note to Myself #1:

I search more efficiently if I underline everything I need to look up, then mark it in some way. For instance, putting an "M" next to everything I want to look up on Mapquest, a "D" next to words I want to look up in a dictionary and a "B" next to everything I want to look up on Biography.com. That way, I can research all the clues that require the use of a particular site at one time.

Note to Myself #2:

When a computer is not available, the mysteries that are assigned to me can be researched with reference books. Even though some facts may not be available in reference books, there are enough details about every suspect to allow me to find some proof of guilt or innocence. I have discovered that the failure to find a fact does not mean that fact is wrong.

Note to Myself #3:

Every mystery I have encountered in my career has fallen into one of three categories—Easy, Intermediate or Difficult.

All of the information I need to solve Easy Mysteries can be found on the following Web sites:

- **Fact Monster.** www.factmonster.com/encyclopedia.html

- **Information Please.** www.infoplease.com

- **Merriam-Webster On-line.** www.m-w.com

- **Mapquest.** www.mapquest.com

- **Biography.com.** www.biography.com

Intermediate Mysteries require a broader search. The sites used in the Easy Mysteries are still useful, but I have to use a search engine like Google or iTools to find information on a wider variety of Web sites.

Sometimes the Difficult Mysteries really have me stumped. They are more difficult to research, and the documents I find are harder to read and understand. While innocent suspects tell the truth, the guilty suspects don't always clearly lie. Instead, they weave a combination of truths, lies and misleading facts into their statements. Some of the hardest mysteries require an extra bit of initiative and intuition on my part. Also, some of the suspects speak languages other than English, so I have to use Babel Fish Translator to understand them.

Note to Myself #4:

Sometimes the cases I am assigned are too easy for someone of my enormous mental abilities. I make the mysteries more challenging by leaving the facts about the suspects' places and dates of birth until last. After I have researched everything else the suspects tell me, I research the birthplaces and dates as a final confirmation of my results. I am almost always right.

Note to Myself #5:

I never pay for information, and I never give out information about myself. If a Web site asks for my name, e-mail address, snail mail address or anything else, I go elsewhere for my information.

Note to Myself #6:

I don't pay attention to banner ads or pop-up ads. I didn't get to be the Research Bureau's best detective by wasting my time on advertisements.

Internet Navigation Manual

First Things First

Internet searches start with a search engine, which is a program that conducts a search for documents on the World Wide Web. While most search engines will return similar results, the order in which the results are listed differs from one search engine to another. Some return information-rich sites high on the result list, while others return commercial shopping sites first. To research the mysteries in this book, the following search engines are particularly useful:

- **iTools.** www.itools.com

iTools consists of a page of search windows labeled Web Search, Web Directory, Find People, Dictionary, Encyclopedia, Biography, Quotations, Text Translator, Web Page Translator, Maptools, etc.

- **Google.** www.google.com

In addition to listing information-rich sites early in the result list, Google has an uncluttered search page that eliminates distractions.

Searching for Web Sites

The best thing about the Internet—the amount and variety of information to which you have access—is also one of its biggest challenges. For instance, suppose you want to find information about cranberries. Typing the key word **cranberries** into the search window of a search engine will result in a list of about 400,000 Web sites, a great many of them for an Irish musical group. You need to use additional key words to narrow the search to Web sites that would be useful to you. **Cranberries plant** will return a list of Web sites about the cranberry plant. **Cranberries plant grow** will return a list of sites about growing the cranberry plant.

Cranberries plant photo will produce Web sites with photos of cranberry plants. Be careful, though. **Cranberries photo** without the word **plant** will produce sites with photos of the Irish band.

Some search engines require the use of an operator in order to link two or more key words. The most commonly used operator, the + sign, directs the search engine to list only Web sites that contain all of your key words. The need for operators varies from one search engine to another. Because Google and iTools ignore the + sign operator, **cranberries + photo + plant** will return the same list of results as the same key words—**cranberries photo plant**—typed in without the + sign. The best rule of thumb is this: When in doubt, try it both ways.

Useful key words to use in a search include: **definition, picture** or **photo, history, biography** or **bio, characteristics, map, birth, death, place** and **date.**

If you cannot think of a key word to use, try writing your search as a question, such as **How many cranberries do U.S. states grow?** Then eliminate all the words you don't need until you have something like **cranberries U.S. states grow.** You can also use an on-line thesaurus to find similar key words. For instance, if you type **grow** into the thesaurus search window of the Merriam-Webster On-line Web site, you will find the words **breed, cultivate, produce, propagate** and **raise,** any of which can be combined with **cranberries** in a search for Web sites.

It is sometimes helpful to do a phrase search, in which the search engine is directed to find words grouped together in a particular order. For instance, **doing an Internet search** will return a list of Web sites featuring all of those individual key words, but those sites won't all be about doing an Internet search.

Putting quotation marks around the phrase "doing an Internet search" will return a far more useful list of sites because it will direct the search engine to find sites in which the words appear in exactly that order.

Because searches depend on machine recognition of words, spelling matters. Typing in **fiends** instead of **friends** will return a list of interesting Web sites, but probably not the ones you were looking for. For the same reason, **cranberry** may result in a different list of sites than **cranberries.** You can maximize your search efficiency by being both accurate and flexible about the key words you use.

After your search results have been reduced to a reasonable number of page titles, take a minute to look down the list. The title of the Web site and the short excerpt showing the way your key words are used in the Web site's text should give you an idea of whether the site might be useful to you.

What's in a Domain Name?

When you seek information from print sources, you can generally judge the accuracy of the information by the publication in which you find it. *The World Book Encyclopedia* is a far more reliable source of information than a supermarket tabloid. The World Wide Web has the equivalent of carefully documented encyclopedias, sleazy slander mills and every variation of accuracy and lunacy in between. Unfortunately, a Web site's appearance will tell you nothing about its accuracy.

One way to assess a Web site is to look at the URL—the address of the site. Especially note the domain name—the suffix at the very end of most addresses. A number of new domain names have recently been approved for use, but right now the most commonly used domain names in the United States are:

- **.com**—Sites maintained by commercial groups. Anyone can have a .com Web site.

- **.net**—Sites maintained by for-profit businesses. Almost anyone can have a .net Web site.

- **.org**—Sites maintained by nonprofit organizations, very often libraries and groups like the American Heart Association.

- **.gov**—Sites maintained by government agencies.

- **.mil**—Sites maintained by the U.S. military.

- **.edu**—Sites maintained by schools, colleges and universities.

In general, sites with **.org, .edu** and **.gov** suffixes provide the most reliable information, but you still need to use your judgment. A **.edu** site can display a fourth-grader's report on oxygen or a complicated analysis of oxygen interaction with nanostructured Ag surfaces. Neither site may be as useful to you as a well-written **.com** encyclopedia site. If you are in doubt about the accuracy of information, look for the information on several different sites and consider the URL suffix in your judgment.

A File by Any Other Name

Sometimes your search will return results that have the symbol [PDF] or the words "File Format: PDF/Acrobat Reader" associated with it. PDF stands for Portable Document Format, which is a program developed by Adobe Systems that allows a document to appear on your computer screen exactly the way it was originally written. Adobe Acrobat Reader is a free program that can be downloaded by clicking on the document you want to open and following the cues to install the program on your computer. Once installed, it will be there to open every other file you encounter that requires Adobe Acrobat Reader. You can also enter the words **Adobe Acrobat Reader** into your search engine's search window in order to access the Web site for installation of the program. Adobe Acrobat Reader is a useful program to have, but Google provides an alternative for those who don't want to install it on their computers. Clicking on the underlined words "View as HTML" next to the search result will take you to a site where the information is presented as text. The HTML will not have the appearance of the original document or some of its charts, graphs and illustrations, but you may still find the information you need there.

A Handy Shortcut

Sometimes a Web site provides too much information for your purpose. For instance, suppose you want to find the names of President George Washington's children without reading through an enormous amount of information about his life. You can use your computer's find function to quickly scan a lengthy text. Start by placing the cursor at the top of the document and pressing the control and "F" keys at the same time. (Press the command and "F" keys on the Mac.) Type **children** into the search window of the pop-up box and click "Find Next." You will be directed to the next use of the word **children** in the document. Continue to click on "Find Next" until you come to the information you want. In this case, you may find that President Washington had no children of his own, but he helped raise his wife's children and two of her grandchildren.

Where to Look for Information

Encyclopedia and Almanacs

- **Fact Monster.** www.factmonster.com/encyclopedia.html

- **Information Please.** www.infoplease.com

Fact Monster and Information Please share the same four on-line resources—an atlas, a dictionary, the Information Please Almanac and Columbia Encyclopedia—but their home pages are designed to appeal to different age groups. Fact Monster is aimed at elementary school students, while Information Please is more appealing to older students. Both sites offer a variety of interesting links, including a Homework Center and features for parents and teachers.

Dictionaries

- **Merriam-Webster On-line.** www.m-w.com

- **Word Central.** www.wordcentral.com

- **Your Dictionary.com.** www.yourdictionary.com

- **Onelook Dictionary Search.** www.onelook.com

Merriam-Webster On-line and its student dictionary version, Word Central, offer a dictionary and thesaurus as well as a word of the day and word games. Your Dictionary.com offers a dictionary, thesaurus and rhyming dictionary. Onelook Dictionary Search is the dictionary to use when you don't know how to spell the word you're looking for. Simply replace letters you're not sure of with an asterisk. For instance, typing **fra*d*l*nt** into the search window will produce the proper spelling of the word "fraudulent." Clicking on the word "fraudulent" will lead to a definition.

Biographical Dictionary

- **Biography.com.** www.biography.com

Biography.com, the on-line version of the A&E television program *Biography*, provides a database of more than 25,000 short, informative biographies of a wide range of people. Names can be entered in either first or last name order, e.g., George Washington or Washington, George.

Atlas

- **Mapquest.** www.mapquest.com

Mapquest is an on-line atlas. To find the location of a city, town, state park, river or natural feature, type the name of the location into the "Get a U.S. Map" search window and fill in the postal abbreviation. (If you don't know the postal abbreviation, click on "state" to see a list.) The resulting map will show the location you want as a red star. You can use your cursor to zoom in or out or move the map east, west, north or south.

Mapquest allows you to map locations in other countries. On the "Map an Address" search page, select a country from the pull-down menu located on the country search window, wait for the screen to change to that country's Mapquest site, then proceed with your location search.

Mapquest can also be used for mapping a route between two locations. Click on Driving Directions and fill in as much information as possible about the beginning and ending points of your journey.

Translators

- **Alta Vista Babel Fish Translator.** babelfish.altavista.com

Babel Fish allows you to write in English, then press a button to have it translated into French, Spanish, German, Portuguese or Italian. It also allows you to do the reverse—enter the words in French, Spanish, German, Portuguese or Italian and translate them into English. Even though the translations are sometimes clumsy and imprecise, this site is very useful.

You can play an amusing on-line form of the old game of Gossip on Babel Fish. Type a sentence like "Twinkle, twinkle, little star, how I wonder what you are" into the search window. Choose the languages to translate from and to, for instance English to French. When you get the French translation, cut and paste it into the search box, then translate from French to German. Follow the same process from German back to English. You will end up with something like this:

"Sparkles, sparkling little star, as I ask myself over, what you is."

Entire Web pages can be translated from one language to another by using the "Translate a Web Page" search window on the Babel Fish site. Simply type in the URL—the Web address—of the site and choose the languages to translate from and to.

Web pages that serve a global audience often have a translation feature, either on the Web site itself or with the page title in the search result list. Suppose your search for Italian wine has returned this possibility: L'Altraguida.com—Antologia Ragionata Del Vino Italiano. You will find the phrase "Translate This Page" beside the page title. Clicking on that option will produce a translated version of the page.

Google also provides a translation service. Clicking on "Language Tools" next to Google's search window will take you to a page that functions just like Babel Fish for text and Web site translations. In addition, Google allows you to search for pages written in any one of 82 languages—including Klingon.

Other Useful Sites

- **Webopedia.** www.webopedia.com

What is the difference between a search engine and a Web browser? What do the letters HTTP at the beginning of a URL mean? For that matter, what does URL mean? Webopedia is a good site to visit for clear answers to questions about computers and the Internet.

- **Urban Legends Reference Pages.** www.snopes.com

The Internet is a virtual barnyard full of Chicken Littles, all of them frantically e-mailing that "the sky is falling!" Women are dying from sniffing perfume samples they have received in the mail. Forward it on! A dying child needs your help to get into the Guinness Book of World Records. Forward it on! A flashing Instant Message means someone is trying to steal your password. Forward it on!

Before you click that e-mail forward button, check the message out on Urban Legends Reference Pages. You will find a large, continuously updated compendium of e-rumors and virus alerts on a site that is also fun to read.

Print Resources Navigation Manual

How to Use Reference Books

It's as Easy as ABC

The telephone book you have in your home is a reference book. It contains useful information—the name, address and phone number of most of the people in your city or town—organized alphabetically. That means that every person whose last name begins with the letter "A" is listed before every person whose last name begins with the letter "B," and so on. A person whose last name is Abell is listed before a person whose last name is Adams (look at the second letter of the names).

In similar fashion, an encyclopedia contains an alphabetical listing of both names and other information. Like the telephone book, it lists people in alphabetical order by their last names. Kennedy, John F. comes after Adams, John Quincy. When last names are the same, first names determine the order, so Kennedy, Benjamin comes before Kennedy, William.

You look up people by their last names in a telephone book, but you wouldn't look up the name of The Great Big Video Store under Store, The Great Big Video even though Store is the last word in the name. You would look it up under the first word of its title—Great. (The words "the" and "a" are usually ignored when they come first in a title.)

Book titles, events, places and objects are listed exactly the same way in an encyclopedia—by the first word of their title. (Remember to ignore "the" and "a" if they are the first word.) The French and Indian Wars comes before Kennedy, John F. in the encyclopedia because "f" comes before "k" in the alphabet. Georgia comes before Juvenile Delinquency for the same reason.

Like a telephone book and an encyclopedia, a dictionary also contains alphabetical listings of information, this time about words and their meanings. But what about an atlas? An atlas usually groups countries together according to which continent they are on, and lists them in order of where they are on that continent. France follows Netherlands and comes before Spain and Portugal, in no particular alphabetical order on an atlas' listing of countries in Europe. Almanacs do not follow alphabetical order either.

Don't panic! A reference book that is not organized alphabetically always has an index, and that index is almost always in alphabetical order. The index can be found at the back of the book in most atlases, or at the front of the book in most almanacs.

Although encyclopedias are arranged alphabetically, they also have an index, usually in a separate volume. An index in an encyclopedia is useful for two reasons:

- It tells you every place in the encyclopedia where the person or event you are researching is mentioned. For instance, according to the index, George Washington is mentioned in 28 separate places in the 2002 edition of *The World Book Encyclopedia.*

- The index tells you where to look for people, places and events that do not have their own listing in the encyclopedia. For instance, you cannot find "Major Richard I. Bong" in the 2002 edition of *The World Book Encyclopedia* unless you use the index. The index tells you that "Bong, Richard I." is mentioned in a listing titled "Ace" on page 24 of Volume A.

Reference Book Shorthand

Because reference books have to pack a lot of information into a limited amount of space, they often use a form of shorthand. Instead of printing "John Tyler was born in 1790 and died in 1862," the encyclopedia might print "Tyler, John (1790–1862)." Sometimes the information is written like this: "b. 1790 d.1862." The "b" stands for year of birth and the "d" stands for year of death. Be careful, though. In some sources John Tyler's name is followed by the dates 1841–1845. Knowing that he was a U.S. president, you should be able to figure out what those years refer to.

Taking Advantage of Shortcuts

When an encyclopedia entry is long, the publishers often include a sidebar—a box containing the most important dates and information. For instance, suppose you are looking for information about George Washington. The information on George Washington in the 2002 edition of *The World Book Encyclopedia* is 19 pages long, but there are several sidebars, one of which lists the most important events in his life. Sometimes the information in the sidebars is enough to answer your questions.

At other times, the information in the sidebars is insufficient. Suppose you want to know how George Washington died. Instead of reading through all 19 pages of his entry, you could be logical about the search. Because a person's death comes at the end of his life, it is logical to guess that information about his death would come at the end of the article. Start your reading a paragraph or two from the end of the article, and see if you find the information there.

There is another way to read quickly through a long encyclopedia entry. Read only the dark print—the headings and subheadings—until you find what you are looking for. If you scan through the entry on George Washington, you would find the heading "First in the Hearts of His Countrymen (1797–1799)" followed by the subheading "Death." By reading the paragraphs that follow that subheading, you would learn the details of George Washington's death.

Where to Look for Information—Print Resources

Almanacs

Almanacs are good places to look for lists and statistics. They contain information about Academy Award, Pulitzer Prize, Nobel Prize and Olympic Game winners; U.S. holidays; inventors and their inventions; major fires, hurricanes and other disasters. They also contain pictures of the flags of every country, short biographies of U.S. presidents, descriptions of the planets in our solar system and information about the 50 U.S. states and major U.S. cities. The index is in the front of most almanacs.

Atlas

Atlases contain maps of the United States and the world. Some atlases include information on the number of people who live in every city listed and a mileage scale that can help you determine the distance between any two points on a map. Some atlases have a complete index in the back of the book, but other atlases have only a general index that refers you to a more detailed index beside each map.

Atlases give map coordinates for each place listed, usually as a number and letter, like "E3." To locate that place on the map, find the letters and numbers at the top and on the side of the page, respectively. Run one finger down the page from "E" and another finger across the page from the "3." The area where your fingers touch is "E3."

Biographical Dictionary

Biographical dictionaries contain information about famous people. Entries here are shorter than those in an encyclopedia. People are listed alphabetically by their last names, just as they are in a phone book.

Dictionary

Dictionaries contain the meanings of words and a guide to their pronunciation. Words are listed alphabetically.

Encyclopedia

Encyclopedias contain information about people, places and events. Information is arranged alphabetically, and most encyclopedias have an index (usually the last volume of the set). The index is useful for locating information that does not have its own listing in one of the main encyclopedia volumes.

Foreign Language Dictionaries

Foreign language dictionaries usually are divided into two sections. One section lists words in another language—for instance, French—and gives the words' translations in English. The second section lists words in English and gives their French translations. Words are listed alphabetically.

Internet Navigation at a Glance

Search Engines

A search engine is a program that searches for Web sites on the World Wide Web. The following search engines are useful for finding reference information:

- **iTools.** www.itools.com
- **Google.** www.google.com

Web Sites

Web sites are the places on the World Wide Web where information is located. The following Web sites are useful:

Encyclopedias and Almanacs

- **Fact Monster.** www.factmonster.com/encyclopedia.html
- **Information Please.** www.infoplease.com

Dictionaries

- **Merriam-Webster Online.** www.m-w.com/home.htm
- **Word Central.** www.wordcentral.com
- **Your Dictionary.com.** www.yourdictionary.com
- **Onelook Dictionary Search.** www.onelook.com

Biographical Dictionary

- **Biography.com.** www.biography.com

Atlas

- **Mapquest.** www.mapquest.com

Translators

- **Alta Vista Babel Fish Translator.** babelfish.altavista.com

Print Resources at a Glance

Almanacs

Almanacs are good places to look for birth and death dates of famous people, statistics about cities and countries, information about major awards and a variety of other lists. The index is in the front of most almanacs.

Atlases

Atlases contain maps of the United States and the world. Some atlases have a complete index in the back of the book, but other atlases have only a general index that refers you to a more detailed index beside each map.

Biographical Dictionaries

Biographical dictionaries contain information about famous people. People are listed alphabetically by their last names.

Dictionaries

Dictionaries contain the meanings of words and a guide to their pronunciation. Words are listed alphabetically.

Encyclopedias

Encyclopedias contain information about people, places and events. Information is arranged alphabetically, and most encyclopedias have an index (usually the last volume of the set.) The index is useful for locating information that does not have its own listing in one of the main encyclopedia volumes.

Foreign Language Dictionaries

Foreign language dictionaries usually are divided into two sections. One section lists words in another language—for instance, French—and gives their definitions in English. The second section lists words in English and gives their French definitions. Words are listed alphabetically.

Detective's Report

Title of the Mystery: _____

(For each suspect, give reasons for your decision on guilt or innocence.)

Suspect 1: _____

Age_____   Guilty_____   Innocent_____

Suspect 2: _____

Age_____   Guilty_____   Innocent_____

Suspect 3: _____

Age_____   Guilty_____   Innocent_____

Suspect 4: _____

Age_____   Guilty_____   Innocent_____

What crime was committed?

How was the crime committed?

Why was the crime committed?

If something was stolen, where is it?

Sample Mystery
The Mystery of the Footloose Fleas

The Crime

Fluffy-Puffy was looking good. Her lovely white and apricot-colored coat was soft as summer clouds. Her breath was minty fresh. She held herself alert, yet regally aloof. The bichon frise was everyone's bet to win the Best in Show ribbon at the prestigious Downtown Dog Show, until she raised her tiny hind foot and scratched behind her ear. The judges, correctly discerning the cause of Fluffy-Puffy's itchy discomfort, ordered her removed, not just from the dog show but from the entire building. "We cannot risk contaminating the other contestants," one of the judges explained. "Fleas are a serious matter to the dog show community. I doubt that Fluffy-Puffy, or any other canine belonging to the same owner, will ever be allowed in the Downtown Dog Show again."

Delores Dogsbody, Fluffy-Puffy's owner, was beside herself at the decision. "Fluffy-Puffy never had a flea before the Downtown Dog Show!" she insisted adamantly. "Look at this! I found this vial on the floor of the waiting room assigned to Fluffy-Puffy. Can you read this tiny writing on the label? It reads S-i-p-h-o-n-a-p-t-e-r-a. The vial is open. You know what that means, don't you? Someone sabotaged Fluffy-Puffy's chances of winning Best in Show. I want you to find out who that was. I want you to bring me his head on a platter! Well, maybe not that," Delores Dogsbody amended quickly. "I'm sorry, I'm very upset right now."

The Question

Who gave Fluffy-Puffy fleas?

The Suspects

Suspect 1—Natasha Sobaka

Natasha Sobaka, participant in the Downtown Dog Show, claims to have been born in Puppy Creek, Arkansas, which is southwest of Beaver Shores, the year that *Julie of the Wolves* won the Newbery Medal.

"Sit, Pushkin! Be a good puppy in front of vistors. He is a borzoi." Natasha Sobaka referred to the tall Russian wolfhound who sat obediently beside the door as she let us into her house. "I named him after the greatest of all Russian poets, Alexander Sergeyevich Pushkin. My father, who was a Russian émigré, read me Pushkin when I was a little girl. The language is in my blood. I am currently reading Pushkin's great historical tragedy *Boris Godunov*, in the Russian language, of course, which is written in the Cyrillic alphabet. Please sit. Would you like tea?"

"That Fluffy-Duffy incident was tragic." Natasha Sobaka shook her head. "Not as tragic as Pushkin's death in a duel he fought to defend his wife's honor, but no one's life is as tragic as a Russian's, is it? And, of course, Fluffy-Duffy is a dog. And her owner is a dreadful woman who has said some very spiteful things about other dogs, including Pushkin. And the dog never deserved to be in contention for a Best in Show ribbon. Anyone who knows dogs knows that. Still, it must feel awful to be so completely humiliated in front of people whose admiration you desire so fervently." Natasha Sobaka's eyes brightened at the thought. "Was Delores Dogsbody completely devastated? Do you know?"

Natasha Sobaka's Alibi: "Oh, I didn't give Fluffy-Duffy a case of fleas." Natasha

Sobaka dismissed the idea with a wave of her ring-bedecked hand. "If I had wanted to wreak vengeance on Delores Dogsbody I would have done something to **her.** Why get innocent dogs involved?"

Suspect 2—Paloma Perro

Paloma Perro, participant in the Downtown Dog Show, claims to have been born in Dog Corner, Maine, which is west of Blackstrap, the year that Nathan Handwerker died.

"Don't mind Sweety. She's friendly." Paloma Perro led us past a tall dog that was making an ominous growling sound deep in its throat. "She's an Ibizan hound. From Ibiza. Of course you know where that is. The island," Paloma Perro prompted when we didn't answer. "Majorca, Minorca, Ibiza—the chief islands of the Balearic Islands, an archipelago off the coast of Spain, in the western part of the Mediterranean. Oh, dear, are they no longer teaching geography in the schools today? Well, never mind. Sit down." She waved her hand in the direction of an ivory-colored couch where Sweety had already made herself at home.

"You've come to ask me what I know about that dreadful Fluffo-Puffo business. The answer is 'nothing.' I saw nothing, heard nothing, know nothing. I mind my own business at those shows. Sweety and I do the best we can and we try not to be disdainful of those little duster doggies, don't we Sweety-weetie." Sweety emitted a barely audible but distinctly unpleasant growl.

Paloma Perro's Alibi: "I was in Sweety's waiting room with her. I don't visit around like some of the contestants do."

Suspect 3—Giovanni Cane

Giovanni Cane, participant in the Downtown Dog Show, claims to have been born in Poopaaelua, Hawaii, which is northeast of Captain Cook, the year that *Dog Soldiers* by Robert Stone won the National Book Award.

"Siphonaptera, you say?" Giovanni Cane responded to our question. "Of course I know what siphonaptera are. They are wingless insects that are parasitic on mammals and birds. They suck blood, just like vampires. Can you imagine having your skin pierced by an insect's mouthpart, then having your blood sucked out like soda through a straw? I feel very sympathetic to Puffy-Fluffy. That poor dog was in a great deal of discomfort. But Delores Dogsbody has no right to accuse any of us of sabotaging her dog's chances of winning Best in Show by giving it fleas. Fleas can survive for weeks without a host and without a blood meal. Perhaps that vial was left behind after the entomologist's convention that took place in the auditorium two weeks ago."

Giovanni Cane's Alibi: "Oh, I was here and there and everywhere. I have a lot of friends at these dog shows. I visit around. It's not about **winning,** you know. It's about being part of something and enjoying oneself. Isn't that right, my pretty Spumone Spinone?" He leaned down to pat a dog that wagged not only its tail, but the entire length of its densely-furred body. "He's a Spinone Italiano," Giovanni Cane explained. "First-rate all-purpose hunting dog, aren't you, *caro mio?*"

Suspect 4—Dudley Dogsbody

Dudley Dogsbody, Delores Dogsbody's husband, claims to have been born in Barkeyville, Pennsylvania, which is south of Whiskerville, the year that Thomas Nashe wrote the play *The Isle of Dogs.*

"I'm not fond of dogs," Dudley Dogsbody said, lowering his voice and casting a nervous glance across his shoulder. "Maybe you shouldn't tell my wife I said that. Fluffy-Puffy's the most important thing in her life. She enters all the dog shows. We're always on the road, traveling from one to the other. It costs a fortune. And I'm not fond of, well, you know ..." He stepped over Fluffy-Puffy's sleeping, snoring body. "I'm a cat person, really. President Clinton had a cat. Mittens, her name was. And George Bush had three cats—Caspar, Melchior and Balthazar. When presidents of the United States choose cats over dogs, I think that tells you something about the habits of successful people. George Washington had a parrot. He called it Polly, which is not terribly creative, but maybe it was a more original name for a parrot when he was president back in 1785."

Dudley Dogsbody's Alibi: "Okay, I'm going to tell you the truth," Dudley Dogsbody said nervously. "Delores left me alone with Fluffy-Puffy because she had to drive home and find his favorite chew toy because, she said, if he didn't have his favorite chew toy he would get anxious and he wouldn't do his best. And I was supposed to brush him and talk to him and sing to him, but mostly I was supposed to safeguard him because my wife thinks everyone is so consumed with jealously about this"—he waved his hand at the prostrate furry form sprawled out on his living room floor—"this poor excuse for a pet that she suspects everyone of malevolent intent. I didn't brush him," Dudley Dogsbody admitted. "And I didn't talk to him or sing to him. I went outside and smoked a cigarette and thought about how wonderful life would be if I never had to attend another dog show in my entire life. Please don't tell my wife I said that."

The Solution

The owners of Fluffy-Puffy's rivals had reasons to dislike Delores Dogsbody. She was suspicious that others were trying to harm her dog and she had said some spiteful things about other dogs in the Downtown Dog Show. But her husband, Dudley Dogsbody, had an even greater reason to sabotage Fluffy-Puffy's chance of winning Best in Show. He was tired of spending money and time on an endless round of competitions. Maybe he brought the vial of fleas with him and waited for a chance to be alone with Fluffy-Puffy, but it is more likely that he found a vial of fleas left behind after the entomologist's convention a few weeks before. Finding himself alone with Fluffy-Puffy and a vial of hungry insects, he made a rash decision that he no doubt would like to keep secret from his wife.

Information About the Suspects

Suspect 1—Natasha Sobaka

- Puppy Creek, Arkansas, is southwest of Beaver Shores, Arkansas.

- *Julie of the Wolves* won the Newbery Medal in 1973.

- The borzoi is also called the Russian wolfhound.

- Alexander Sergeyevich Pushkin is considered by many Russians to be the greatest Russian poet who ever lived. His 1831 novel *Boris Godunov* is an historical tragedy.

- Alexander Pushkin died fighting a duel to defend his wife's honor.

- The Russian language uses the Cyrillic alphabet.

Suspect 2—Paloma Perro

- Dog Corner, Maine, is west of Blackstrap, Maine.

- Nathan Handwerker, creator of Nathan's Famous Hot Dogs, died in 1974.

- The Ibizan hound, or Ibizan Podenco, comes from the Balearic Islands. Majorca, Minorca and Ibiza are the chief islands of the Balearic Islands, which are located off the coast of Spain, in the western part of the Mediterranean.

Suspect 3—Giovanni Cane

- Poopaaelua, Hawaii, is northeast of Captain Cook, Hawaii.

- *Dog Soldiers* by Robert Stone won the National Book Award in 1975.

- Siphonaptera, also known as fleas, are wingless insects that are parasitic on mammals and birds. Their mouth parts pierce their host's skin, then they suck their host's blood.

- Fleas can survive for weeks without a host and without a blood meal.

- The Spinone Italiano is a hunting dog.

Suspect 4—Dudley Dogsbody

- Barkeyville, Pennsylvania, is northwest, not south, of Whiskerville, Pennsylvania.

- Thomas Nashe wrote the play *The Isle of Dogs* in 1597.

- President Clinton's cat was named Socks. He also had a dog named Buddy.

- President George W. Bush entered the White House with two cats, Ernie and India. He also had two dogs, Spot and Barney.

- George Washington had a parrot, which he called Polly, but he was not president of the United States until 1789.

Easy Mysteries

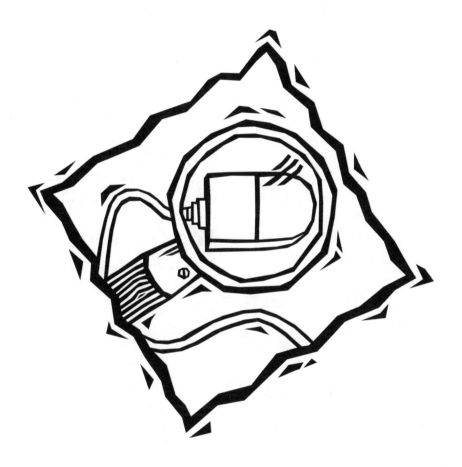

The Mystery of the Stolen Santa Suit

The Crime

Gus Grimley is not in a holiday mood. He had opened his costume shop on Christmas Eve because a potential customer wanted to rent a Santa Claus costume, but the red suit wasn't there. It was hanging on the rack, brushed and neat, the following morning, but Gus is absolutely certain it wasn't there on Christmas Eve.

"I lost money," Gus said indignantly. "The customer was so desperate to have the suit I could have charged double my normal rental rate, so I lost at least $90. I want that money back!"

The Question

Who borrowed the Santa suit on Christmas Eve?

The Suspects

Suspect 1—Brother Darius

Brother Darius, who runs the Downtown Ecumenical Mission and Soup Kitchen next door to Gus Grimley's Costume Shop, claims to have been born in Santa Claus, Georgia, which is west of Ohoopee, the year that *Baboushka and the Three Kings* won the Caldecott Medal.

"The Three Wise Men who visited Jesus in the stable were Magi," Brother Darius told us. "They were members of the priestly caste of Ancient Persia. Some scholars believe they were leaders of the Zoroastrian faith. Because they were thought to have power over demons, the word 'magi' gave rise to the word 'magic.' And that's what I believe happened on Christmas Eve. A Santa Claus suit was spirited out of Gus Grimley's store, and the next morning poor families all over this neighborhood found presents waiting for them. It was a Christmas miracle in the spirit of the Three Magi, praise the Lord!"

Brother Darius's Alibi: "I was in my room behind the soup kitchen praying for the Gus Grimleys of this world to throw off the shackles of soul-oppressing consumerism so they can revel in the plenitude of God's omnipresent love."

Suspect 2—Danny Delinquo

Danny Delinquo, who lives with his aunt and uncle in a small apartment above Gus Grimley's Costume Shop, claims to have been born in Ho-ho-kus, New Jersey, which is northwest of Yonkers, three years after Tim Allen made the movie *The Santa Clause.*

"I didn't do it!" Danny Delinquo said defensively. "I'm glad something bad happened to him, but I didn't do it this time. Did he say I did it? He hates me. You know what he calls me? He calls me 'Mistletoe' because, he says, I'm a parasite on my aunt and uncle, just like the real mistletoe plant that sticks its roots into a host plant to suck out water and food."

"Brother Darius says not to listen to the 'embittered wretches of this world,'" Danny Delinquo continued. "Brother Darius told me that the mistletoe was considered a sacred plant by the Druids, and that a lot of people back in olden times thought it cured their sicknesses. He said maybe the nickname 'Mistletoe' is a message that I am being called to help people. You think he might be right?"

Danny Delinquo's Alibi: "I was asleep. Before I went to bed I prayed that my aunt and uncle would get presents. And you know what?" His face brightened. "The next morning, there were presents in the hallway. There were two for me! There was something for everyone in the building except for Mr. Grimley."

Suspect 3—Leslie Lightouch

Leslie Lightouch, who lives in an apartment across the street from Gus Grimley's Costume Shop, claims to have been born in Dasher, Georgia, which is south of Herring, the year that Claus Sluter died.

"So Gus the Cuss lost money," Leslie Lightouch chuckled as he led us into a minuscule apartment made even less commodious by stacks of tape recorders, boom boxes and CD players. "I pick things up here and there," he said, explaining the mess. "I engage in 'consumer goods reallocation' and I make no apology for it, especially around the holidays. It's like Brother Darius says, 'An excess of possessions blinds a man to joy,' so I do what I can to help men see."

"I love everything about Christmas," he said, redirecting our attention. "I love the lights and giving presents, but I especially like the music. I love every Christmas carol ever written, but I'm extremely partial to the music of Bing Crosby, maybe because his real first name was Leslie, just like mine. His rendition of 'White Christmas' just blew me off my feet when it first came out in 1955."

Leslie Lightouch's Alibi: "Could I have picked Gus Grimley's lock?" Leslie Lightouch laughed. "Anyone could have picked it. He was too cheap to install a decent lock. But I was right here in my apartment listening to Bing croon 'Silent Night.' Funny thing, though. I was looking out my window and I saw a guy dressed up like Santa Claus walking down the street. I thought that was a great idea."

Suspect 4—Roland Polynski

Roland Polynski, who is known to his elementary school students as Mr. Roly-Poly, claims to have been born in Rudolph, Wisconsin, which is east of Vesper, the year that Gian-Carlo Menotti's opera, *Amahl and the Night Visitors,* premiered on television.

"Yeah, I know who I look like." Roland Polynski stroked his full white beard. "Even when I was young, I looked like that guy. The American version of him," he was quick to add. "The one that Clement Clarke Moore described in his poem 'A Visit From St. Nicholas,' which was published in 1823. The original Saint Nicholas—the one who was probably a bishop in Asia Minor in the fourth century—was quite a different character. There are a few legends about him that would give squeamish children nightmares."

Roland Polynski's Alibi: "Don't let this get around, okay?" His cheeks flushed as pink as roses. "I do something special on Christmas Eve. I get dressed up as Santa Claus and go around the neighborhood leaving presents for the children and their families. They're good people. They deserve a visit from Santa Claus. But I didn't need to borrow a costume from Gus Grimley's shop," he continued. "I have my own. I'd show it to you, but I sent it to the cleaners."

The Mystery of the Stolen Santa Suit

The Solution

Danny Delinquo received two presents from Santa Claus because there were two Santas in the neighborhood that night. Leslie Lightouch waited until Roland Polynski had finished making his gift-giving rounds, then Leslie slipped out to do his own "consumer goods reallocation." He had admired Roland's costume, so he took a few extra minutes to pick the lock on Gus Grimley's Costume Shop and borrow a Santa suit for himself.

Information About the Suspects

Suspect 1—Brother Darius

- Santa Claus, Georgia, is west of Ohoopee, Georgia.

- *Baboushka and the Three Kings* won the Caldecott Medal in 1961.

- The Three Wise Men were Magi, members of the priestly caste of Ancient Persia, whom some scholars believe to have been leaders of the Zoroastrian faith.

- The word "magic" came from "magi."

Suspect 2—Danny Delinquo

- Ho-ho-kus, New Jersey, is northwest of Yonkers, New Jersey.

- Tim Allen made the movie *The Santa Clause* in 1994. Danny Delinquo was born three years later, in 1997.

- The mistletoe plant is partially parasitic, but it was considered sacred by the Druids because it was believed capable of curing illness.

Suspect 3—Leslie Lightouch

- Dasher, Georgia, is northwest, not south, of Herring, Georgia.

- Claus Sluter died around 1405.

- Bing Crosby's original name was Harry Lillis Crosby, not Leslie Crosby.

- "White Christmas" was introduced in the movie *Holiday Inn*, which was released in 1942.

Suspect 3—Roland Polynski

- Rudolph, Wisconsin, is east of Vesper, Wisconsin.

- Gian-Carlo Menotti's opera, *Amahl and the Night Visitors,* premiered on television December 24, 1951.

- Clement Clarke Moore described a rosy-cheeked, chubby, jolly Santa Claus in his poem "A Visit From St. Nicholas." It was written in 1822 and published in 1823.

- The original Saint Nicholas was probably a bishop in Asia Minor in the fourth century.

The Mystery of the Heisted O'Henry Bars

The Crime

It seemed like a great idea. Since the O'Henry candy bar had been named after baseball great Hank Aaron, why not raise money for the sports department by selling O'Henry bars to students during Verdant Valley High School's big baseball rally? Coach Lefty Longwood had been offered a good deal on 100 cases of the confection from the school's office supply delivery man. He paid for the product with money from the athletic department's Bat and Ball Account and took delivery behind the gym. Unfortunately, while he was trying to find a few strong students to carry the boxes inside, the candy disappeared.

The Question

Who stole the O'Henry bars?

The Suspects

Suspect 1—Lou Gehrig Pulaski

Lou Gehrig Pulaski, Verdant Valley High School's band director, claims to have been born in Baseball Park, Indiana, which is east of Fredsville, 30 years after Lou Gehrig Appreciation Day was held in Yankee Stadium.

"That's how I got my name," he told us. "My father was there that day. He was only six years old, but he never forgot how Lou Gehrig got up to speak to the crowd. This powerhouse of a ball player, this man who had been part of a New York Yankees line-up so formidable it was called Murderers' Row, was dying of a horrible disease called amyotrophic lateral sclerosis. He would be dead before his thirty-eighth birthday. But you know what he said? He said, 'I consider myself the luckiest man on Earth.' According to Dad, there wasn't a dry eye in the stadium that day. That man had class."

"Unlike Coach Lefty," he confided. "The coach is always looking to make a few quick bucks or cut corners in some way. He doesn't know the meaning of the word 'integrity.' When I saw those candy boxes stacked up behind the gym I knew he had been up to one of his schemes and I thought it would be great if someone taught him a lesson. But I wasn't the one who did it," Lou Gehrig Pulaski added emphatically. "I grew up with 'The Iron Horse' as my role model. I don't lie or steal."

Lou Gehrig Pulaski's Alibi: "I was in the band room tuning the tubas."

Suspect 2—Delilah "Deli" Counter

Delilah "Deli" Counter, Verdant Valley High School's dietitian, claims to have been born in Pitcher, New York, southeast of East Homer, the year *One Fine Day* won the Caldecott Medal.

"I don't mind all this silliness about the baseball season," she told us as she swept through the school's cafeteria like the doyenne of dinner tables. "As a matter of fact, I knew Catfish Hunter personally. My grandparents lived near his family farm in Hertford, North Carolina, and Catfish himself showed me the hole in the barn door through which he pitched balls to practice his accuracy. He was a very nice man. I was very sad to hear that he died a few years back of that same awful disease that killed Lou Gehrig. I prepared a culinary homage to him the day of the rally—Verdant Valley Catfish Surprise."

"No, it's not the baseball rallies or any of the other sports-related hoopla that steams my pudding," Deli Counter rattled on. "It's the idea of selling candy bars to students in the name of athletics and good health! What on earth does Coach Lefty have between his ears? When I saw those boxes behind the gym I thought, 'Someone ought to get rid of all those empty calories before students put them into their perfectly lovely bodies.'"

"But I didn't do it!" Deli Counter added, shaking a stainless steel industrial-size spatula in our direction. "If you even suggest that possibility I will turn you into next week's Verdant Valley Mystery Meat Surprise."

Delilah "Deli" Counter's Alibi: "I was in the cafeteria perfecting my recipe for Succotash Surprise."

Suspect 3—Peter Pilferton

Peter Pilferton, delivery driver for School Office Supply Company, Inc., claims to have been born in Diamond, Alabama, east of Hustleville, the year that Joseph Jefferson Jackson was banned from playing professional baseball.

"This delivery gig is just a temporary job," Peter Pilferton told us. "Until I can get enough money together to make a demo record. Then I'll make it big. I make a little extra money on the side, picking up a few things here, selling them to a few people there. Like the principal, who buys my reconditioned copy machine ink cartridges to save a few bucks on his office supply costs and the ladies in the office who are always interested in jewelry. I got a good deal on the O'Henry bars because they'd been sitting in a warehouse for a few years and were a bit on the stale side, but who's going to notice something like that, right? So Coach Lefty, he wants them at the price I quote him, everybody's happy."

Peter Pilferton's Alibi: "I was in the office chatting with the ladies about this baseball ballyhoo. No disrespect to Hank Aaron, but I'm a Babe Ruth man myself. He learned to play ball at St. Dominick's School for Boys in New York City, which is my alma mater, then he went on to become the King of Home Run Hitters. I cried like a baby the day that man died. Interestingly, he died of the same horrible disease that killed Lou Gehrig."

"Anyway, when I went back to my truck I was surprised to see the cartons of candy bars sitting all by their lonesome outside the gym door. Where I grew up, a guy who turned his back on his stuff didn't get his stuff back, if you know what I mean."

Suspect 4—Bartholomew "Batty" Brown

Bartholomew "Batty" Brown, assistant athletic coach at Verdant Valley High School, claims to have been born in Catcher, Arizona, which is northwest of Diamond Grove, the year that Jackie Robinson died.

"Looks bad for the coach, doesn't it?" Batty Brown said with undisguised glee. "He does an unauthorized transfer of funds from an athletic account to buy old candy bars for an unsanctioned fundraiser, and now everything's gone. Poof! That's not going to look good to the school committee. Maybe they'll fire him this time."

"I was against this candy sale from the start. I was against using Hank Aaron to make money off the kids. Jackie Robinson was the first African American to play in the major leagues, but Hank Aaron was one of the first African American baseball players to move into a major league front office, into the business and recruitment end of the game. That was a significant accomplishment, too. That's the kind of thing I'm always thinking about," Batty Brown continued. "How to get ahead, career-wise, and how to help others get ahead. That's why I would be a much better coach for these kids than Longwood is."

Bartholomew "Batty" Brown's Alibi: "I was hiding in the last place the coach would ever go—the school library. I knew he was looking for someone to move all of those cartons, and I didn't feel like being his toady for the day. Did anybody see me? I don't know. Everyone was getting ready for the baseball rally, so the place was empty. Even the librarian was gone."

The Solution

Peter Pilferton grew up where the philosophy was simple: "A guy who turned his back on his stuff didn't get his stuff back." When he saw the cartons of O'Henry bars sitting unattended outside the gym he quickly loaded them back into his delivery truck. It probably didn't take a long time before stale candy bars went on sale at another school along Pilferton's route.

Information About the Suspects

Suspect 1—Lou Gehrig Pulaski

- Baseball Park, Indiana, is east of Fredsville, Indiana.

- During Lou Gehrig Appreciation Day, which was held in Yankee Stadium on July 4, 1939, Gehrig said, "I consider myself the luckiest man on Earth." Lou Gehrig Pulaski was born 30 years later, in 1969.

- Lou Gehrig was part of a New York Yankees lineup called Murderers' Row.

- Gehrig died of amyotrophic lateral sclerosis two weeks before his thirty-eighth birthday. The disease has come to be known as Lou Gehrig's Disease.

Suspect 2—Delilah "Deli" Counter

- Pitcher, New York, is southeast of East Homer, New York.

- *One Fine Day* won the Caldecott Medal in 1972.

- Catfish Hunter grew up on a farm in Hertford, North Carolina. He practiced his pitching accuracy by throwing balls through a hole in a barn door.

- Hunter died of amyotrophic lateral sclerosis, also known as Lou Gehrig's Disease, the same illness that killed Lou Gehrig.

Suspect 3—Peter Pilferton

- Diamond, Alabama, is west, not east, of Hustleville, Alabama.

- Joseph Jefferson Jackson ("Shoeless Joe") was banned from playing professional baseball in 1921.

- Babe Ruth learned to play baseball at St. Mary's Industrial School for Boys in Baltimore, not at St. Dominick's in New York City.

- Babe Ruth died of cancer, not amyotrophic lateral sclerosis.

Suspect 4—Bartholomew "Batty" Brown

- Catcher, Arizona, is northwest of Diamond Grove, Arizona.

- Jackie Robinson died in 1972.

- Jackie Robinson was the first African American to play in baseball's major leagues.

- Hank Aaron was one of the first African American baseball players to move into a major league front office, into the business and recruitment end of the game.

The Mystery of the Purloined Presents

The Crime

It may have been Reginald Ronald Rooney's fourth marriage, but it was his blushing bride's first, and she wanted the wedding of her dreams. A rented chateau, bowls of rare orchids on every table, a dozen ice sculpture swans cradling bowls of caviar between their wings, hundreds of white doves released into the air the moment the wedding vows were exchanged—nothing was too extravagant for Mitzy Muldooney and her 500 guests.

Unfortunately, extravagance does not guarantee perfection. The father of the bride went missing just before the wedding, so Mitzy had to walk down the aisle without him. The overexcited doves voided on the bridesmaids. While the food was delicious, there wasn't enough of it for all the guests. Even more upsetting, while the bride and groom were saying their "I do's" in front of the frangipani-ringed duck pond, dozens of expensive wedding gifts disappeared from the chateau's Gift Display Room.

The Question

Who stole the Muldooney-Rooney wedding presents?

The Suspects

Suspect 1—Michael "Big Mike" Muldooney

Michael "Big Mike" Muldooney, father of the bride, claims to have been born in Weddington, North Carolina, which is north of Stallings, the year that Prince Albert married his first cousin.

"You're going to find this out anyway, so I might as well be straight with you. I've gone bust," Big Mike Muldooney confessed. "My construction company had a bad year. There were some cost overruns. I made some bad investments. I don't have the money to pay for a wedding like this."

"I thought I'd faint when Mitzy told me what that fancy French fashion designer, Viollet-le-Duc, was charging for the wedding dress. And she can't go to Las Vegas for the honeymoon. That's too 'jejune,' she says. She needs to go to Kiribati. I'm so 'jejune' myself that I didn't even know where Kiribati was until she told me it's the capital of Senegal, and then I didn't bother to tell her I don't know where Senegal is, either."

"But never mind," Big Mike Muldooney sighed heavily. "Mitzy is my baby girl. I never could say no to her. I'll find some way to pay for the wedding."

Michael "Big Mike" Muldooney's Alibi: "Honestly? I was in the driveway throwing up into the bushes. My chauffeur was there with my SUV. He'll corroborate my story."

Suspect 2—Father Desmond

Father Desmond, pastor of St. Bride's of the Bowery, claims to have been born in Bridal Veil, Oregon, which is east of Troutdale, the year that Jerry Falwell married Macel Pate.

"You noticed that I was out of place there, did you?" Father Desmond asked rhetorically. "I believe that Mitzy Muldooney-Rooney chose me to officiate at her wedding because she liked the sound of my church's name—St. Bride's of the Bowery. She certainly has no knowledge of the original St. Bride—St. Bridget of Ireland—who was associated with both charity and justice. Neither of these qualities were in evidence at the Muldooney-Rooney nuptials."

"I did not take umbrage at the fact that the donation I received for performing the ceremony was less than the cost of one bowl of caviar at the reception," Father Desmond continued. "I turned the other cheek when the bride insisted that her father rent me a decent suit for the wedding because my own clothing was not acceptable. But I'm afraid I succumbed to impatient and unseemly thoughts when she refused to let the two young assistants I brought with me attend the reception. She said, 'We might not have enough food for my guests to have seconds.'" Father Desmond's eyes snapped angrily. "She said that in front of two young people who do not always eat three meals a day."

Father Desmond's Alibi: "I confess that I continued with the ceremony despite my anger because I hoped the father of the bride would make a generous contribution to my parish. Alas, that did not happen. He turned out to be as stingy as his daughter is rude. I told my two assistants to wait for me in the car, and I bought them a good meal on the way home."

Suspect 3—Candace Dandridge

Candace Dandridge, owner of Candy Is Dandy Caterers, claims to have been born in Wife Lead, New York, which is south of Freeport, the year that Martha Kostyra married Andy Stewart.

"When you've been in business as long as I have, you know who's going to stiff you on the bill," Candace Dandridge told us bluntly. "Every time his daughter decided that the champagne ought to be a better, more expensive brand, Big Mike would break into a sweat. Not that Mitzy Muldooney had enough of a brain in her head to know what she wanted," Candace Dandridge laughed unpleasantly. "She told me that Reggie wanted 'the champagne discovered by that monk, Don Corleone.' She was referring, of course, to Dom Perignon, the monk who reputedly developed the process for making champagne back in the seventeenth century. When she said, 'I want you to make sure there's none of that dangerous carbonic acid in it,' I nearly burst out laughing. The sparkle in champagne comes from the carbonic acid content. I remember thinking that after a few months with Mitzy the groom would probably be happy to drink cyanide."

Candace Dandridge's Alibi: "I was in the kitchen, stealing from my client," Candace Dandridge told us candidly. "Earlier that afternoon, when I asked Big Mike for the final payment, he patted his jacket and made a big deal about being surprised that he had forgotten his wallet. I knew I was going to take a big loss on this job. So I had my employees pull the catering vans up to the house. We loaded them up with all the food I thought I could freeze and use at another function. Big Mike can have the hors d'oeuvres when he pays for them."

Suspect 4—Delores Bitterly

Delores Bitterly, formerly Delores Rooney, claims to have been born in Husband, Pennsylvania, which is northwest of Somerset, the year that Donald Trump married Ivana Zelnickova Winklmayr.

"I was wife number two," Delores Bitterly admitted. "Wife number one manages an apartment complex. Wife number three works at the mall. We meet occasionally for lunch to compare notes on what we have in common. We all had a bit of money before Reggie the Rat entered our lives; we all ended up broke," Delores Bitterly enumerated. "And none of us has ever received a dime of alimony."

Delores Bitterly's Alibi: "I'll tell you the truth, since I think Mike Muldooney probably told you anyway. I was in the Gift Display Room. I was curious to see what Reggie was going to get out of this marriage. There was a lot of silver. And Tiffany glass," she sighed. "There was a favrile glass vase just like one I used to own. My vase was designed by Louis Comfort Tiffany around 1900. That was one of the many beautiful possessions I had to sell to pay my debts."

"I thought about stealing it," Delores Bitterly confessed. "It would have been easy enough. A french door opened directly onto the circular driveway and a pair of cypress trees restricted the view from other entrances. But then I saw Mr. Muldooney puking into the shrubbery. He looked up and saw me, then Candace called me to help with loading the catering vans. I don't know whether I would have stolen the vase or not," she said candidly. "The question is moot now, isn't it?"

The Solution

Poor Big Mike. He couldn't say no to anything Mitzy wanted, but he couldn't pay for her extravagant whims, either. His frazzled nerves, and perhaps a bit of Dom Perignon, made him ill. When he had finished upchucking into the shrubbery he looked up. He noticed Delores in the Gift Display Room, and he realized the same thing she had—it would be very easy to steal the gifts. He and his chauffeur carried the wedding presents out through the french doors and loaded them into his SUV. He intended to sell them later and use the money to pay the wedding bills.

Information About the Suspects

Suspect 1—Michael "Big Mike" Muldooney

- Weddington, North Carolina, is southwest, not north, of Stallings, North Carolina.

- Prince Albert married his first cousin, Queen Victoria of England, in 1840.

- Viollet-le-Duc was an architect, not a dress designer.

- Kiribati is an island nation in the South Pacific.

- Senegal is in Africa.

Suspect 2—Father Desmond

- Bridal Veil, Oregon, is east of Troutdale, Oregon.

- Jerry Falwell married Macel Pate in 1958.

- St. Bride, also known as St. Bridget of Ireland, was associated with both charity and justice.

Suspect 3—Candace Dandridge

- Wife Lead, New York, is south of Freeport, New York.

- Martha Kostyra married Andy Stewart in 1961.

- Dom Perignon, a monk, reputedly developed the process for making champagne in the seventeenth century.

- The sparkle in champagne comes from carbonic acid.

Suspect 4—Delores Bitterly

- Husband, Pennsylvania, is northwest of Somerset, Pennsylvania.

- Donald Trump married Ivana Zelnickova Winklmayr in 1977.

- Louis Comfort Tiffany patented a process for making favrile glass in 1894. He made vases.

The Mystery of the Flaming Forest

The Crime

Snowy Mountain Ski Resort was a possible site for the next Winter Olympics until a fast-moving fire roared up the mountainside, devouring all the bone-dry tinder in its path. Now that its ski trails are flanked by blackened stubs of evergreens, no one wants to ski there. Snowy Mountain Ski Resort is closed and bankrupt.

The Question

Who started the fire that ruined Snowy Mountain Ski Resort?

The Suspects

Suspect 1—Sven Svarn Svenson

Sven Svarn Svenson, owner of a rival ski resort, claims to have been born in Burns, Colorado, which is southwest of Copper Spur, the year that Sonja Henie made the movie *Sun Valley Serenade*.

"I attended the Winter Olympics in 1960, when they were held in Squaw Valley, California, and again in 1980, when they were held for the second time in Lake Placid, New York," Sven Svarn Svenson told us. "So I was familiar with the kind of accommodations and security an event like the Winter Olympics requires. It was ridiculous of the Snowy Mountain people to think they could provide what was needed, but that didn't stop them from applying. And it didn't stop them from spreading rumors in order to knock my ski resort out of consideration." Svenson's jaw muscles tightened with anger. "They spread rumors about my cooks using coyote in the chili, about bed bugs in the mattresses and, most seriously, about my ski lifts and trails being inadequately maintained. I rather enjoyed the fire," he admitted with a smile. "I was evacuated by helicopter, so I got a good look at it from above."

Sven Svarn Svenson's Alibi: "I have no alibi whatsoever. I was hiking on the mountain, checking out the condition of Snowy Mountain's lifts and trails. But you need more evidence than that to accuse me of arson."

Suspect 2—Frederick "Sparky" Ash

Frederick "Sparky" Ash, a member of the Snowy Mountain Volunteer Firefighting Brigade, claims to have been born in Burnsville, Minnesota, which is west of Savage, the year that Garrett A. Morgan patented his "breathing device" hood.

"I was born to fight fires," Sparky Ash told us enthusiastically. "I, like, totally identify with my hero, Red Adair. I mean, like, here's this guy who's born filthy rich, right? He could be chairman of the board of his daddy's oil company, but he walks away from that in order to be, like, the most audacious fire dude on the face of this planet. I mean, back in the early '90s when he capped the Devil's Cigarette Lighter that had been sending up a pillar of flame for months over there in Liberia, I thought, whoa, this guy is, like, Superman or something. That's what I want to do. I want to be like Red Adair. I want to prove what I can do, know what I mean?"

Frederick "Sparky" Ash's Alibi: "I was poking around in the woods looking at bugs with my pocket magnifying glass and wishing something exciting would happen in this place before my brain shriveled to the size of a, you know, peanut or something. Then I smelled smoke and I knew it wasn't just a campfire. I have, like, an instinct for fire, you know what I mean? And I ran down the mountain to give the alarm and came back up with the guys to fight it. Too bad about the ski resort." Sparky Ash shrugged. "I thought we were going to be able to contain the blaze, but the wind came up and it got away from us, you know?"

Suspect 3—Valentino Banderas

Valentino Banderas, whose legal name is Stanley Fritterhoffer, claims to have been born in Fire Island Pines, New York, which is south of Bohemia, the year that Earth, Wind & Fire released their album *Electric Universe*.

"I named myself after two of my heroes, because I feel myself to be like them," Valentino Banderas told us in an Italian accent that was not totally convincing. "I was Snowy Mountain Ski Resort's most popular ski instructor, especially with the women. Then I was fired. They said it was because I misrepresented my affections and intentions with the female clients, but that wasn't the real reason," Valentino Banderas insisted. "The owner found a letter I may have written to his wife. It was harmless, but what can I do in the face of jealousy?"

"Now the owner is sorry." Banderas smiled unpleasantly. "He tells everyone that the resort has gone bankrupt because of the fire, but the truth is that the clients no longer come because I am no longer there. They came to Snowy Mountain to see Valentino Banderas. Me."

Valentino Banderas's Alibi: "I was in my cabin at the base of Snowy Mountain rereading a biography of Rudolph Valentino. I had just come to my favorite part, Valentino's funeral. When his female fans learned that he had died of a perforated ulcer, some of them attempted suicide. I was so engrossed in the book I didn't realize at first that the wood smoke smell wasn't coming from my fireplace. I barely escaped with my life."

Suspect 4—Nya Eva Northrup

Nya Eva Northrup, a waitress at Snowy Mountain Ski Resort before the fire, claims to have been born in Burns Harbor, Indiana, which is north of Portage, the year that John Jackson Sparkman died.

"I loved Valentino!" Nya Eva Northrup said, wiping away a tear. "And I thought he loved me, too. He wrote me beautiful letters saying that I was like the soft breeze of spring across a frozen Earth. He compared me to Venus, the Roman goddess of vegetation, and to Gaea, the Greek goddess of the earth. No one had ever said things like that to me before. Then I found out that other women had received the exact same letters! He wrote them on a word processor and printed them out by the ream!"

"I burned his letters in a campfire I built in the woods. I think the fire might have been my fault," she confessed. "After I burned the letters I cried so much I fell asleep from exhaustion. When I woke up, my campfire was out, but I could smell smoke. I think a spark from my campfire might have drifted up into the pines on the mountain above me. I never intended to hurt anyone! I'm so sorry!" Nya Eva Northrup sobbed.

Nya Eva Northrup's Alibi: "I think I started the fire. I'm willing to accept the consequences. If I can't have his love, I might as well be in prison anyway. Or a nunnery." She broke into sobs again. "A quiet cloister would be nice."

The Solution

Frederick "Sparky" Ash was bored with life on Snowy Mountain. He longed for a chance to be a firefighter like his hero Red Adair. So he started a little blaze with his pocket magnifying glass. Maybe the first small wisp of flame was an accident—let's give him the benefit of the doubt—but he didn't put it out. He ran down the mountain to give the alarm and rally his fellow firefighters. Before they could get back to the fire with their equipment the blaze was bigger than Frederick "Sparky" Ash had expected. They couldn't extinguish it in time to save the ski resort.

Information About the Suspects

Suspect—Sven Svarn Svenson

- Burns, Colorado, is southwest of Copper Spur, Colorado.

- Sonja Henie made the movie *Sun Valley Serenade* in 1941.

- The Winter Olympics were held in Squaw Valley, California, in 1960, and in Lake Placid, New York, in 1932 and 1980.

Suspect 2—Frederick "Sparky" Ash

- Burnsville, Minnesota, is east, not west, of Savage, Minnesota.

- Garrett A. Morgan patented his "breathing device" hood in 1914.

- Red Adair came from a poor family. He did cap the Devil's Cigarette Lighter, but that fire occurred in Algeria in 1962, not Liberia in the early '90s.

Suspect 3—Valentino Banderas

- Fire Island Pines, New York, is south of Bohemia, New York.

- Earth, Wind & Fire released their album *Electric Universe* in 1983.

- Rudolph Valentino died of a perforated ulcer. Some of his female fans reportedly attempted suicide.

Suspect 4—Nya Eva Northrup

- Burns Harbor, Indiana, is north of Portage, Indiana.

- John Jackson Sparkman died in 1985.

- Venus was the Roman goddess of vegetation.

- Gaea was the Greek goddess of the earth.

The Mystery of the Dreadful Dwelling

The Crime

Norman Normal and his family had lived in Eden's Acres Perfect Planned Community for less than a month when their new reproduction of a turn-of-the-century Victorian house began to experience problems. A clogged pipe in the second-floor bathroom sink caused an overflow that sent water cascading down the hallway stairs. The floors had barely dried from that mishap when the garbage disposal screeched and smoked and stopped working altogether. Little more than a week later a short circuit in the basement wiring created a spark that ignited a pile of newspapers in the recycling bin. Fortunately, Norman Normal was close enough to extinguish the fire before it got out of hand. The final straw was an invasion of field mice. Norman Normal demanded that the Eden's Acres Perfect Planned Community Association refund the money he had paid for the house.

Not so fast, the Eden's Acres Perfect Planned Community Association responded. The clog in the upstairs bathroom had been caused by a wad of cloth that had been rammed into the pipe. The garbage disposal's motor had burned out when the appliance jammed on a mixture of corn cobs and pebbles. The basement wiring had been tampered with, and the mice were the type that came from a pet store, not a field. Someone had been causing deliberate damage to the house, and the Eden's Acres Perfect Planned Community Association wasn't refunding anyone a dime.

The Question

Who caused the damage to the Normal family's new house?

The Suspects

Suspect 1—Norman Normal

Norman Normal, head of the Normal family, claims to have been born in Normal, Kentucky, east of Getaway, the year that Etienne Cabet died.

"Buying this house was a huge mistake," Norman Normal admitted as he sat in the middle of his basement recreation room controlling the speed and course of several miniature trains. "Everything is planned here. Everything is perfect. That sounded good until I got here and realized how many rules there are. The trash goes out on Monday mornings, no earlier than four, no later than seven, and must be in the bins provided by the Eden's Acres Perfect Planned Community Association. Cars must be kept in the driveway during the day and in the garage at night. Curtains must be drawn back during the day and lowered at night. The rules go on and on."

"One morning I woke up and realized that I don't want order and predictability," Norman Normal said. "I want adventure. See that train over there with the blue locomotive and the blue rail cars? That's a model of the Blue Train, also known as the Orient Express, which runs from Istanbul to Moscow. It ascends to 13,000 feet to cross the Alps, making it the world's highest railway. It goes so high that there are doctors aboard to administer oxygen to passengers who get altitude sickness. That's what I want. I would give up all the safety and convenience of the Eden's Acres Perfect Planned Community for the chance to experience altitude sickness on one of the world's greatest trains."

Norman Normal's Alibi: "The Eden's Acres Perfect Planned Community Association is trying to blame me for the defects in this house, but they can't prove anything," Norman Normal asserted. "I was here in the basement when the fire started, and it's lucky I was—otherwise my family might have burned to death—but I wasn't even in the state when the garbage disposal burned out. I was at an electrical engineers' convention in Las Vegas. And I was at my office when the upstairs sink overflowed."

Suspect 2—Naomi Normal

Naomi Normal, Norman's wife, claims to have been born in Normal, Alabama, which is south of Dug Hill, the year that Stephen Pearl Andrews died.

"Come inside, quickly!" Naomi Normal insisted, closing the door behind us. "The Eden's Acres Perfect Planned Community Association is watching us. They're such horrible, horrible people. I don't know how we could have been so thoroughly fooled by them when we looked at this community. It seemed so wonderful. They promised that everything would always be neat and orderly and friendly. It would be like living in an American small town of the early 1900s, but with lots of twenty-first-century appliances. But the community isn't fun. It's like something out of a horror movie. Everyone is supposed to do what the Eden's Acres Perfect Planned Community Association tells them to do."

"I wanted to create a garden," Naomi Normal told us. "A nice vegetable garden. I wanted to plant turnips—the white ones, *Brassica blanca,* and the yellow ones,

Brassica verdura, which you probably know by the name of kohlrabi. And corn. Oh my, I so love corn freshly picked from the garden. But the minute I put a spade into the earth, someone from the Eden's Acres Perfect Planned Community Association appeared with a list of **approved** plants for our yard. It is a very short list." Naomi frowned. "Roses. Pink. Shrub-size. That's all. Not even **red** roses. Not even **rambling** roses. They have to be **pink, shrub** roses. I'm going to go insane if we can't get out of here."

Naomi Normal's Alibi: "Of course I was in the kitchen when the garbage disposal burned out! I'm the housewife around here! I'm always in the kitchen! But I had nothing to do with that disaster, or any of the others, either, especially the mice. I hate mice! I would never touch a rodent. The Eden's Acres Perfect Planned Community Association is trying to make us responsible for damage caused by defects in their workmanship. They are wretched, horrible people."

Suspect 3—Nellie Normal

Nellie Normal, Norman and Naomi's daughter, claims to have been born in Normal, Tennessee, which is north of Rugby, the year that Amos Bronson Alcott died.

"This place makes me want to puke," Nellie Normal said with disconcerting frankness. "I hate it so much my bones ache with hating it, even when I'm asleep. I used to play hockey in my old hometown. You know, ice hockey, in a rink with eight players on a team—a goalie, a center, four defensemen and two forwards. I was a defenseman," she said proudly. "But they don't have a rink here. The Eden's Acres Perfect Planned

Community Association doesn't even allow kids to play street hockey. It's too rough, someone might get hurt. And it isn't ladylike," she added with a derisive snort. "They suggested I take a baton twirling course at the Community Recreation Hall. As if!"

Nellie Normal's Alibi: "If I had started a fire in this house I would have made sure no one was around to put it out," Nellie Normal promised. "This place is like going to Hell without dying first. I kind of like the mice, though."

Suspect 4—Ninuccia "Nonna" Normale

Ninuccia "Nonna" Normale, Norman's mother, claims to have been born in Little Italy, Arkansas, which is west of Wye, the year that Christian Metz was born.

"This is a bad place." Nonna Normale shook her head sadly. "Especially for an old woman like me. Where I used to live, I played mah-jongg every Tuesday and Thursday with my friends. I have my own mah-jongg set. Look. Isn't it beautiful?" she asked, opening a box to reveal rows of wood and ivory tiles. "There are 200 tiles in every set—50 wind tiles, 50 dragon tiles, 50 flower tiles, 40 water tiles and 10 joker tiles, which we refer to as grand jongg tiles. It's a very simple game, very sociable. But there is no mah-jongg game here," Nonna Normale sighed. "When I offered to start a mah-jongg group at the Community Recreation Hall, the Eden's Acres Perfect Planned Community Association said that there were enough activities already. They suggested that I join a seniorcise class. See-nyour-cise!" Nonna Normale enunciated the word derisively. "What is that? Exercise for old people? Why don't they just call it exercise? Do they call the class they want my daughter-in-law to join middle-ager-cise?"

Ninuccia "Nonna" Normale's Alibi: "What are you asking? You think a little old lady like me goes around starting fires and playing with mice? As for the garbage disposal, I don't trust modern gadgets. I don't even use the washing machine. I do up my undies by hand."

The Solution

There is one nice thing to be said about the Eden's Acres Perfect Planned Community Association. It united the entire Normal family behind a single goal—to escape from the Eden's Acres Perfect Planned Community.

Norman Normal wasn't home for the clogged pipe or ruined garbage disposal debacles, but he was certainly there when fire broke out in the basement. He knew enough about wiring to create the spark that ignited the newspapers, and he knew enough about the dangers of fire to quickly put it out. He wasn't concerned about the house going up in a conflagration, but he was far too good a father to subject his family to that kind of danger.

Although Naomi Normal knew what corn cobs and a few pebbles would do to a garbage disposal, she would never touch a rodent. But Nellie would. The Normal daughter was the family member most likely to buy mice at a pet store and release them in the house. And sweet old Nonna? Well, there were those undies she washed up in the sink.

They all had one purpose—to prove the house defective so they could get their money back from the Eden's Acres Perfect Planned Community Association.

Information About the Suspects

Suspect 1—Norman Normal

- Normal, Kentucky, is southwest, not east, of Getaway, Kentucky.

- Etienne Cabet died in 1856.

- The Blue Train runs between Cape Town and Praetoria, South Africa.

- The Orient Express runs between Paris, France, and Istanbul, Turkey.

- The Peruvian Central Railway is considered to be the world's highest railway, ascending to more than 13,000 feet to cross the continental divide. Doctors ride the Peruvian Central Railway to administer oxygen to passengers suffering from altitude sickness.

Suspect 2—Naomi Normal

- Normal, Alabama, is northwest, not south, of Dug Hill, Alabama.

- Stephen Pearl Andrews died in 1886.

- White turnips are known by the scientific name *Brassica rapa*.

- Yellow turnips, *Brassica napobrassica*, are popularly known as rutabagas.

Suspect 3—Nellie Normal

- Normal, Tennessee, is southeast, not north, of Rugby, Tennessee.

- Amos Bronson Alcott died in 1888.

- There are six players on a regulation ice hockey team: a goalie, a center, two defensemen and two forwards.

Suspect 4—Ninuccia "Nonna" Normale

- Little Italy, Arkansas, is east, not west, of Wye, Arkansas.

- Christian Metz was born in 1794.

- As mah-jongg is currently played, a mah-jongg set includes 152 tiles (small rectangular pieces of wood with ivory or bone faces), divided into the following categories: 108 suit tiles, 16 wind tiles, 12 dragon tiles, 8 flower tiles and 8 jokers. The three suits are bamboo (sticks), circles (dots) and characters (cracks).

- Mah-jongg is a complicated game.

The Mystery of the Misplaced Missive

The Crime

Ida Bea Sweet, fifth-grade teacher at Loving Neighbors Elementary School, does not regret what she did when she won the state's 10 million dollar lottery. She packed a suitcase and spent the summer touring Europe's greatest cities. However, she does regret that she left too expeditiously to pay attention to her mail. "I shoved it all into a shoebox," Ida Bea explained. "When I got back from my trip and went through it, I found this."

This was a love letter. "I have adored you since our eyes first touched as lightly as the wings of butterflies dancing above a morning meadow," it read. "But my courage has failed to follow where my heart has bade it fly." It went on in similar fashion for two full pages, extolling the beauty of Ida Bea Sweet's eyes, ears, nose, mouth and elbows, and comparing her to, among other things, Aphrodite, the morning sunrise, and dew on newly-blossomed roses. It quoted Shakespeare, the Bible and dozens of poets. The only thing the letter failed to contain was a signature or return address.

"This letter was written before anyone knew I had won the lottery," Ida Bea Sweet pointed out. "I want to know who loved me when I was a poor elementary school teacher. And I want to know if he still loves me now."

The Question

Which suspects are lying about writing the love letter? Who wrote the love letter to Ida Bea Sweet?

The Suspects

Suspect 1—Edward U. Kater

Edward U. Kater, principal of Loving Neighbors Elementary School, claims to have been born in Love, Illinois, which is south of Hooppole, the year that Elijah Parish Lovejoy died.

"I wrote the letter to Ida Bea," Edward U. Kater readily confessed. "I was reluctant to say anything because I was the principal and I didn't want to create an awkward situation if she didn't return my feelings, though I felt sure she would. We feel the same way about so many things, especially education. Public education is"—he made a sour face—"futile, really. Students have too much freedom. There are too few expectations. How can young people learn to **be** accountable in a system that doesn't **hold** them accountable?"

"If I had enough money I would start my own educational academy," Edward U. Kater confided. "It would be based on the principles of the famous British educator John Dewey, who felt that schools should teach the classics to all children. Latin, Greek, the canon of western literature," Edward U. Kater enumerated. "John Dewey was such a brilliant man that, while he was establishing a system of public schools in England and Scotland, he still had time to invent the Dewey Decimal System. The man knew the importance of order and discipline. He's my personal hero."

Edward U. Kater's Alibi: "I wrote the letter and I placed it in Ida Bea's school mailbox on the last day of school. No one saw me do it."

Suspect 2—Moore Braun

Moore Braun, physical education teacher at Loving Neighbors Elementary School, claims to have been born in Love Place, Arizona, which is north of Fortune, the year that Jack Lovelock was born.

"Of course I wrote the letter!" Moore Braun bristled with irritation. "Are you one of those people who think a physical education teacher can't express himself in literate prose? I wanted to show Ida Bea that I am a man of both words and action. My dream is to run the Olympic marathon and dedicate my run to her. I heard that Ida Bea went to Marathon, Greece, where it all started back in A.D. 490 when Menander ran from Marathon to Sparta to announce the need for more troops. That was the run that the first modern Olympic marathon event in 1902 was patterned after. I dream of seeing Marathon, Greece, and running in the Boston Marathon and having the best equipment so I can train for the Olympics. And spending my life with Ida Bea. I have a lot of dreams beating here inside my handsome chest."

Moore Braun's Alibi: "I slipped the letter into Ida Bea's school mailbox when no one else was looking. I didn't understand why she didn't answer as soon as she read it, but I realize now what happened. That was careless of her, but I wholeheartedly forgive her for making me wait with such anxious uncertainty."

Suspect 3—John D. Bree

John D. Bree, custodian at Loving Neighbors Elementary School, claims to have been born in Love, Mississippi, which is north of Robinson Gin, the year that Augusta Ada King, the Countess of Lovelace, died.

"I loved that woman from the very first moment she started a recycling project in her classroom," John D. Bree informed us as he patrolled the school yard looking for litter. "It's like I said to Ida Bea, there's no such thing as trash. There's just stuff that hasn't found its recycled use yet. Broken glass, for instance. I collect all of it I can find because my brother and I are going to start a recycled glass business as soon as we get enough capital to buy equipment. We're going to specialize in producing water glass. You've never heard of the stuff? It's that really strong glass that gets used in the big aquariums. It's actually 50 or 60 sheets of glass fused together, and it has to be especially crystal clear to cut down on distortion. I used to talk to Ida Bea about my plans, and I could tell that she was as fascinated by glass production as I am."

John D. Bree's Alibi: "Yeah, I wrote the letter. I put it in her school mailbox on the last day of classes, then I hid in the boiler room. I was nervous, I guess. You tell Ida Bea that I've loved her since her classroom recycling project. It would be fantastic if she'd consent to be my wife. Tell her I have a sister who makes wedding gowns out of recycled plastic."

Suspect 4—Peter Pater

Peter Pater, father of one of Ida Bea Sweet's students, claims to have been born in Love, Kentucky, which is east of Eden, the year that Esther Pohl Lovejoy died.

"I'm a bit abashed about the letter," Peter Pater admitted as he led us into a small art studio where he produces greeting cards. "I was working on a line of Valentine cards at the time. I combine a realistic art style with historical facts, like these that show Saint Valentine as he might have looked before his martyrdom in A.D. 270. Or these street scenes of Terni, a town in the Umbria section of Italy that claims to have been the original home of Saint Valentine. So much thinking about the man who came to be the patron saint of those unhappily in love made me maudlin. Not that I didn't mean everything I said in the letter," Peter Pater hastened to add. "I just never intended for that wonderful woman to see the letter. I had no reason to believe she'd return my feelings, and I still have little to offer her," he admitted. "I eke out a modest living with my greeting cards, though I have enough faith in my talent to think that I could be successful if I had an infusion of money to increase production and widen distribution."

Peter Pater's Explanation: "My son, P. J., has confessed to me that he found the letter in my studio and slipped it into Ms. Sweet's school mailbox when he took the morning attendance sheet to the school secretary. P. J. is as crazy about Ms. Sweet as I am."

The Solution

Ida Bea Sweet has become the dream girl of Loving Neighbors Elementary School. Edward U. Kater dreams of their life together and the school he can build with her lottery winnings. Moore Braun dreams of seeing Marathon, Greece, running in the Boston Marathon, training for the Olympics and, oh yes, spending his life with Ida Bea. John D. Bree dreams of running a glass manufacturing business with his brother, and Peter Pater dreams of expanding his greeting card business. However, Peter Pater also dreamed of Ida Bea's eyes, ears, nose, mouth and elbows before she won the lottery. He wrote his feelings down, never intending to send the letter. But P. J. Pater found the love letter in his father's studio and decided to slip it into Ida Bea Sweet's school mailbox.

Information About the Suspects

Suspect 1—Edward U. Kater

- Love, Illinois, is northeast, not south, of Hooppole, Illinois.

- Elijah Parish Lovejoy died in 1837.

- John Dewey was an American philosopher and educator who believed that schools should change to reflect the society around them. While he consulted in other countries, he did not establish a system of public schools in England and Scotland.

- Melvil Dewey, a librarian, invented the Dewey Decimal system.

Suspect 2—Moore Braun

- Love Place, Arizona, is south, not north, of Fortune, Arizona.

- Jack Lovelock was born in 1910.

- The marathon, a long-distance foot race, is patterned after the run of Pheidippides from Marathon, Greece, to Athens to announce the news that the Greeks had defeated the Persian army in 490 B.C. A commemorative event traced the route of the original run in the first modern Olympics held in Greece in 1896. In 1908 the race became an Olympic event.

- Menander was a Greek poet and playwright.

Suspect 3—John D. Bree

- Love, Mississippi, is south, not north, of Robinson Gin, Mississippi.

- Augusta Ada King, the Countess of Lovelace, died in 1852.

- Water glass, a soluble glass available in powder or liquid form, is used as a detergent, a cement for fixing glass or pottery, a fixative in pigments for paint or cloth and a protective coating for eggs. It is not used for aquarium windows because, being soluble, it will eventually dissolve in water.

Suspect 4—Peter Pater

- Love, Kentucky, is east of Eden, Kentucky.

- Esther Pohl Lovejoy died in 1967.

- Saint Valentine, an early Roman priest, was martyred in A.D. 270 or 269. Terni, a town in the Umbria section of Italy, claims to be the original home of Saint Valentine. He is popularly considered to be the patron saint of lovers and those who are unhappily in love.

The Mystery of the Monsters in the Ravine

The Crime

Sasquatch and cyclops and chupacabras ... Oh, my!

Hank, Frank, Linda, Lucy, Marty, Arty, Corrine, Lorrinda, John, Jennie, Mitzy-Lou and at least a half dozen other children in the hamlet of Rustlers Refuge have heard about the frightening creatures who inhabit the ravine at the edge of town. "Horrible things slide through the shadows," Hank confided in a frightened whisper. "I don't like talking about them. If they hear us say their names, they'll come for us at night."

"Everybody knows about them," Lorrinda added. "The grown-ups told us about the creatures. Grown-ups don't lie, do they?"

"Most of us stay away from the ravine," Marty said. "But Frank and John and Mitzy-Lou have been there."

"It was creepy," John admitted. "We heard rustling sounds in the bushes and something grabbed Mitzy-Lou's shirt."

"Just reached out and grabbed me," Mitzy-Lou concurred. "I still have the rip in my favorite Britney Spears shirt where it tried to get me."

"You'd have to be crazy to go into the ravine," Lucy said adamantly. "If we don't bother the monsters, they won't come after us. I hope." The other children nodded their agreement.

The Question

Who has been scaring the children of Rustlers Refuge?

The Suspects

Suspect 1—Louis "Loopy Lou" LaMotta

Louis "Loopy Lou" LaMotta claims to have been born in Mount Savage, Maryland, which is south of Slabtown, the year that Hieronymous Bosch died.

"I come out here every few days to tend my field of hemp plants, you know, *Cannabis sativa,*" he said, gesturing to the handsome foliage that rustled in the summer breeze. "Hemp goes into making rope, you know. My father was a farmer, too, so I guess this way of life is in my blood."

Louis "Loopy Lou" LaMotta's Alibi: "Yeah, I've heard some of those stories," he admitted with a laugh. "There was a real good one about zombies—you know, those flying monkey creatures who steal babies out of their cradles—but I don't remember where I heard it. You know," he added seriously, "if the kids have been scared away from the ravine, that's a good thing, 'cause there's things down here that could hurt a kid if he ain't careful. You know?"

Suspect 2—Herbert "Hooch" Hoover

Herbert "Hooch" Hoover claims to have been born in Ghouls Fork, North Carolina, which is north of Blades, the year that Emperor Hongwu died.

"I come out here every few nights because I love all things about the natural world," Hooch Hoover said, gesturing toward the canopy of densely interlaced tree branches above him. "I love my

mountain dew. I love the white lightning this area produces on a soft summer night. I love the moonshine. Beautiful, beautiful moonshine," he crooned to the trees. "How I love ya, how I love ya, my dear old moonshine ..."

Herbert "Hooch" Hoover's Alibi: "Stories?" His eyes snapped back into focus. "Have I been telling the local kids wild stories? Let me think." He scratched his head in contemplation. "I've got a pretty good one about the time I saw the Yeti out in Washington state when I was married to my second wife. Or maybe it was my third wife. I don't always remember details too well."

"If I said something—and I'm not sure if I did or didn't—I never meant to scare anyone. Though it'd be good if they stayed out of this ravine. There aren't any good reasons for kids to be playing down here when they have a perfectly good playground behind their school."

Suspect 3—Prudence Planter

Prudence Planter claims to have been born in Casper, Wyoming, which is south of Goose Egg, the year the author of *Frankenstein* died.

"I consider myself a horticultural archivist," she said as she led us on a tour of her cottage garden. "I find wildflowers and herbs in the ravine, transplant them to my garden and study them. I support my academic endeavors by selling some of the plants I find in the ravine to home gardeners and wildflower enthusiasts around the country. That's the trailing arbutus," she explained as we bent down

The Mystery of the Monsters in the Ravine

to examine a patch of glossy green vegetation. "It's such a common wildflower it's this state's flower. There's a lot of it in the ravine."

Prudence Planter's Alibi: "Stories?" Prudence Planter snorted derisively. "I don't believe in filling children's heads with nonsense, though I might have mentioned something about the hematophagous tendencies of the vampire bats that are so prevalent in North American deciduous forests. In my opinion, it is not a bad thing that the children are frightened of the ravine. I don't know what kind of parent would allow a child to play in such a dangerous place, anyway."

Suspect 4—Frederick "Fishman" Fontana

Frederick "Fishman" Fontana, claims to have been born in Kill Devil Hills, North Carolina, which is east of Whalebone, the year the author of *Dracula* died.

"I make my living catching fish for the home aquarium trade," Fishman Fontana said as he led us down a steep, crumbling path to a brook that ran through the ravine. "Mostly guppies and mollies, which are small varieties of perch. You might have heard that there are snail darters down here, too. They're actually mollusks, not fish, and they're slimy, but some of my customers want them for their aquariums. There's a customer for almost everything, I guess."

Frederick "Fishman" Fontana's Alibi: "I might be guilty of scaring the children. I'm sorry if I did," he said contritely. "I was trading tall tales with Loopy Lou and Hooch on the porch of the Dew Drop Inn a few weeks ago and I got carried away with my tale about Cerberus—the lion with three heads from Roman mythology. I almost scared myself telling it. Tell those kids I was only fooling, and I'm sorry. But, hey!" He called after us. "Tell them to stay out of the ravine anyway. It's no place for young people to be playing!"

The Solution

Rustlers Refuge Ravine is a busy place. Loopy Lou LaMotta is growing a field of marijuana; Hooch Hoover is distilling illegal alcohol; Prudence Planter is digging up protected* trailing arbutus plants for sale to wildflower enthusiasts; and Fishman Fontana is scooping up protected snail darters for sale to home aquarium owners. None of them want children snooping around in the ravine. All of them have used the power of storytelling to protect their illegal activities from inadvertent discovery.

(* If the trailing arbutus is the state flower, Prudence is in Massachusetts, and if Prudence is in Massachusetts, the trailing arbutus is a protected plant.)

Information About the Suspects

Suspect 1—Louis "Loopy Lou" LaMotta

- Mount Savage, Maryland, is north, not south, of Slabtown, Maryland.

- Hieronymous Bosch died in 1516.

- *Cannabis sativa* plants can supply hemp to make rope, but they are grown mostly to provide the drug marijuana.

- Zombies are not flying monkey creatures that steal babies out of their cradles. They are corpses brought back to life by magic spells.

Suspect 2—Herbert "Hooch" Hoover

- Ghouls Fork, North Carolina, is south, not north, of Blades, North Carolina.

- Emperor Hongwu died in 1398.

- Mountain dew, white lightning and moonshine are all names for alcohol that has been illegally distilled without the payment of federal tax.

- The Yeti is associated with the Himalayas, not the state of Washington.

Suspect 3—Prudence Planter

- Casper, Wyoming, is northeast, not south, of Goose Egg, Wyoming.

- Mary Wollstonecraft Shelley, the author of *Frankenstein,* died in 1851.

- The trailing arbutus is the state flower of Massachusetts, where it is protected by law.

- Vampire bats live in the tropics, not in deciduous forests of North America.

Suspect 4—Frederick "Fishman" Fontana

- Kill Devil Hills, North Carolina, is north, not east, of Whalebone, North Carolina.

- Bram Stoker, the author of *Dracula,* died in 1912.

- Guppies and mollies are killifish, not perch.

- Snail darters are fish, not mollusks.

- Cerberus, a dog with many heads, is a creature from Greek, not Roman, mythology.

The Mystery of the Clobbered Clock

The Crime

The Acme Insurance Company was proud of the clock tower on its new office building. "As forward-looking as the company itself!" press releases touted the digital clock face that loomed three stories above surrounding buildings. "No more boring boings!" the company promised. Indeed, the hourly chimes that characterized clocks of the past had been replaced by "appropriate to the now" digital music. "Wake Up, Little Susie" wafted from the clock tower at 7 a.m. "You Are My Sunshine" played when sensors on the clock tower indicated a warm and sunny day. "Raindrops Keep Falling on My Head" rang out on dark and dreary afternoons. Sometimes the clock played "How Much Is That Doggie in the Window?" for no apparent reason.

So neighbors were annoyed but not alarmed when a mid-morning digital rendition of the "1812 Overture" ended with a loud "Kaboom!" Only when silence accompanied the next few turns of the hour did the president of Acme Insurance Company call a tech-help consultant to investigate. What the consultant found was a small but effective hole blown out of the clock tower's music synthesizer. Lab results point to a home-made bomb containing sulfuric acid.

The Question

Who stopped the music?

The Suspects

Suspect 1—Hiram Hower Glass

Hiram Hower Glass, retired Navy SEAL and amateur clockmaker, claims to have been born in Clockville, New York, which is northeast of Bingley, the year that Robert Donat won the Academy Award for Best Actor in *Goodbye, Mr. Chips*.

"Did I like the Acme atrocity? No!" Hiram Hower Glass said emphatically. "The clock was a garish monstrosity, without style or finesse. Do you know what clocks are about? They're about **time.** Each click of a second hand measures a breath of movement from womb to tomb. Take a look at this beautiful clepsydra." He waved his hand to indicate a silver container that dripped water into a glass vessel beneath it. "Time is measured by the water level in the glass receptacle," he explained. "Clepsydras may have been used in Egypt as early as 2000 B.C., and they were most certainly used in ancient Greece and Rome. Beautiful, beautiful, beautiful ..." he sighed. "Not like that hideously glowering red eye of a clock and its jarring music."

"Do I know how to make a simple bomb?" Hiram Hower Glass looked amused. "My dear child, I was a Navy SEAL."

Hiram Hower Glass's Alibi: "I was right here in my clock room working on a lovely little antique timepiece I purchased recently on eBay."

Suspect 2—Marty Morpheus

Marty Morpheus, who works nights for a 24-hour emergency towing service, claims to have been born in Time, Illinois, which is west of Montezuma, the year that *A Wrinkle in Time* won the Newbery Medal.

"The clock! That spawn of Satan, you mean! That **thing** that waits until I am a half second away from a sound slumber, then blares 'You Ain't Nothin' But a Hound Dog' loud enough to wake the dead! Did I dislike **that** clock? What kind of brain-deficient, idiotic question is that? I'm sorry, I'm sorry, I'm sorry," Marty Morpheus muttered semi-coherently. "I've been sleep-deprived so long I've gotten irritable."

"I work at night, so I need to sleep during the day. You have no idea how important sleep is. Not just catnaps, either. A person needs to go through all four stages of sleep, including REM sleep. That's rapid eye movement sleep," Marty Morpheus explained. "That's the part of the sleep cycle when dreams occur. I haven't had a good dream since that good-for-nothing clock got installed in the Acme building. Until today. The silence is so wonderful. I was right in the middle of a lovely dream when you knocked on my door. What was it you wanted?" he asked blearily.

"Do I have access to sulfuric acid? I don't know. I guess I do. That's what they use in car batteries, isn't it?"

Marty Morpheus's Alibi: "I was trying to sleep. Can I get back to bed now?"

Suspect 3—Grace Vampira

Grace Vampira, owner of Grace's Great Guano Fertilizer, Inc., claims to have been born in Timesville, Texas, which is between Sand Flats and Saint Paul, the year that Jeffrey P. Bezos was born.

"The clock was a trial for all the neighbors," Grace Vampira admitted. "Even for my little sweethearts. You can't see them in the daylight, but they're here in my yard, roosting in the trees and under the eaves of the garage. The ones I have here are members of the Vespertilionidae family—the plain-nosed bats. I especially love the little brown bat, though it doesn't produce enough droppings for my fertilizer company."

"My fertilizer composting and packaging factory is located in New Mexico," Grace Vampira informed us. "The *Tadarida brasiliensis*, the Mexican freetail bat, which roosts in huge numbers in the caverns there, produces an enormous quantity of guano. I was down there just a week ago conferring with my company chemists."

"I know sulfuric acid is used in the manufacture of fertilizer," Grace Vampira admitted, "But I wouldn't have a clue how to use it to blow something up. Besides, a loud explosion would have disturbed my darlings. I don't like anything to disturb their sleep."

Grace Vampira's Alibi: "I was on the phone to the manager of my factory when I heard that ungodly boom. I was very annoyed. Music is one thing, but booms and bongs and kabooms are quite another. I was going to direct my attorney to draft a cease and desist letter to the president of Acme, but I guess the problem has been solved now, hasn't it?"

Suspect 4—Solomon Stringfellow

Solomon Stringfellow, violinist with the Acme City Orchestra, claims to have been born in Times Corner, Indiana, which is south of Saturn, the year that Igor Stravinsky wrote "Fireworks."

"The noise was unbearable," Solomon Stringfellow said seriously. "I'm not referring to the decibel level. I'm referring to the quality of the sound. The clock tower employed a MIDI technology—I'm sure you know that stands for Musician Initiated Digitized Interface—that allowed the computer to control the selection of digitally recorded songs being played. It was mechanically clever, but it was electronic music, not real music. Musicians know the difference. To someone who loves the sound produced when a bow caresses the strings of a violin or a breath resonates in a wooden chamber, that caterwauling clock tower was not a musical instrument. It was more like the demented stepsister of a toaster."

"Could I have built a sulfuric acid-based bomb? Probably," Solomon Stringfellow answered honestly. "Sulfuric acid isn't hard to come by, and neither are bomb-making instructions. Unfortunately."

Solomon Stringfellow's Alibi: "I was home practicing the 'Violin Concerto in D' by Johannes Brahms. It's just as popular with audiences today as it was when it was written back in 1825. The '1812 Overture' interrupted my concentration at first, but the clock was mercifully silent after that."

The Solution

When Solomon Stringfellow said, "Sulfuric acid isn't hard to come by, and neither are bomb-making instructions," he knew what he was talking about. Tired of having his violin practice interrupted by the caterwauling of a "demented stepsister of a toaster," he found a source for sulfuric acid (perhaps a car battery, as Marty Morpheus suggested) and instructions for making a small bomb. Stringfellow walked into the Acme Insurance Building while it was open for business and found the computer room. Since he knew a bit about MIDI technology, he knew where to plant the bomb to do the most harm.

Information About the Suspects

Suspect 1—Hiram Hower Glass

- Clockville, New York, is northeast of Bingley, New York.

- Robert Donat won the Academy Award for Best Actor in *Goodbye, Mr. Chips* in 1939.

- Clepsydras are water clocks. They may have been used in Egypt as early as 2000 B.C., and they were most certainly used in ancient Greece and Rome.

Suspect 2—Marty Morpheus

- Time, Illinois, is west of Montezuma, Illinois.

- *A Wrinkle in Time* won the Newbery Medal in 1963.

- Sleep deprivation can cause personality changes and irritability.

- There are four stages of sleep.

- REM sleep, which stands for rapid eye movement sleep, is the part of the sleep cycle when dreams occur.

- Sulfuric acid is used in car batteries.

Suspect 3—Grace Vampira

- Timesville, Texas, is between Sand Flats and Saint Paul, Texas.

- Jeffrey P. Bezos was born in 1964.

- The plain-nosed bats belong to the Vespertilionidae family. The little brown bat is a plain-nosed bat.

- The *Tadarida brasiliensis*, the Mexican freetail bat, roosts in large numbers in caverns in New Mexico. The bats produce a large quantity of guano.

- Sulfuric acid is used in the manufacture of some fertilizer.

Suspect 4—Solomon Stringfellow

- Times Corner, Indiana, is northeast, not south, of Saturn.

- Igor Stravinsky wrote "Fireworks" in 1908.

- MIDI is an acronym for Musical Instrument Digital Interface, not Musician Initiated Digitized Interface.

- "Violin Concerto in D" was written by Johannes Brahms in 1878, not 1825. Johannes Brahms wasn't even born until 1833.

Intermediate Mysteries

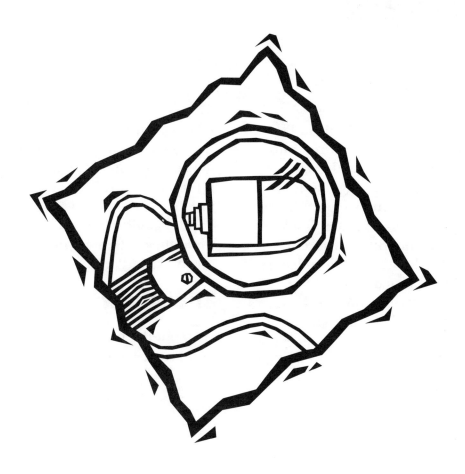

The Mystery of the Piscine Pillagers

The Crime

Something sinister is happening at Placid Pond. There are no more bullfrog calls on summer nights. Ducks and geese have fled. Fishermen haven't caught a fish there in months, although a few fishermen have reported having their hooks struck and bitten off. Biologists from a local university who have studied changes in the pond have issued a disturbing report. A pair of carnivorous northern snakehead fish have been introduced into the pond, and they have eaten everything they've found alive. Even more disturbing is the information that snakehead fish can crawl on land and live for days out of water. The biologists fear that if they are not caught and killed, the fish will head for Pleasant Pond, Pacific Pond, Paradise Pond and Pretty Pond when they have exhausted the food supply in Placid Pond.

The Question

Who put the northern snakehead fish into Placid Pond?

The Suspects

Suspect 1—Robert "Bull" Butman

Robert "Bull" Butman, a construction foreman, claims to have been born in Fish Creek, Wisconsin, which is between Egg Harbor and Sister Bay, the year that *Don't Go Near the Water* by William Brinkley was published.

"I know the biologists are upset, but this silence seems like Heaven to me," Bull Butman told us. "There used to be bullfrogs out there. I'm talking about those big guys, the ones that have legs that are almost 10 inches long. *Rana catesbeiana,* the biologists at the university called them when I contacted them about exterminating them. The males have a loud, booming call—sounds like a bass player with only one string—and boy, did they go at it on summer nights. Jug-a-rum ... jug-a-rum ... jug-a-rum. It was a nightmare. Even with the windows closed I couldn't sleep."

"You know what those biologists told me?" Bull demanded. "They said Placid Pond is on state land and those frogs have every right to be there, even if they're keeping me from getting a decent night's sleep. Some country, huh? When frogs have more rights than a working guy like me. Well, now when those bullfrogs call they're not attracting mates, they're attracting dinner guests."

Robert "Bull" Butman's Alibi: "Oh, sure, I used to go over to the pond and glare at the bullfrogs every once in a while. But I never heard of northern snakehead fish before now. I wish I had."

Suspect 2—Long Yu Tang

Long Yu Tang, proprietor of a Chinese restaurant, claims to have been born in Whitefish, Montana, which is between Lupfer and Halfmoon, the year that Laurence Fishburne was born.

"Okay, I know what a northern snakehead fish is. Do you think that makes me guilty of throwing a pair of them into Placid Pond?" Long Yu Tang asked angrily. "I make a very good watercress soup with northern snakehead fish, dried duck gizzard and candied dates. I serve it to my family for Chinese New Year, which is celebrated on the first day of the first moon of the Chinese lunar calendar, so it falls somewhere between January 21 and February 19. I make the soup if I can get the ingredients," Long Yu Tang amended. "It is sometimes difficult to get good Asian ingredients out here in the boondocks."

"I keep carp in that tank," Long Yu Tang explained as we wandered over to his restaurant's aquarium. "But I'm considering getting a few northern snakehead fish. They are delicious. In the Asian culture their flesh is believed to have curative powers. And curiosity alone would bring in customers," he added. "I am thinking of creating a dish called Scary Ugly Fish With Five Spices. The trouble is, I can't keep carp and snakeheads in the same tank. The carp would disappear."

Long Yu Tang's Alibi: "Why would I put northern snakeheads into Placid Pond? If I had had them, I would have cooked them."

Suspect 3—Blake Fishman

Blake Fishman, student, claims to have been born in Spearfish, South Dakota, which is south of Crook City, the year that Izaak Walton died.

"Do you want to see my aquarium?" Blake asked as he led us to his bedroom overlooking Placid Pond. "I only have one fish right now. It's an *Electrophorus electricus* from somewhere in South Africa. Mauritania, I think. My dad brings me fish from his business trips. This one freaks my mother out because it looks like a snake," Blake admitted. "But it's not dangerous. It produces a low-level energy that helps it detect nearby objects, sort of like bats do. It's not like it could kill anything. I hope it doesn't get much bigger because I won't be able to keep it if it does. My mom says I can have only one aquarium this size and no more. It's not fair, but Dad says there's no sense in arguing with Mom."

Blake Fishman's Alibi: "I've been trying to catch the northern snakeheads, but I haven't had any luck. Anyway," Blake said with a shrug, "it wouldn't be a good idea to put them in the same tank as my electric eel."

Suspect 4—Bryan DePalma

Bryan DePalma, amateur filmmaker, claims to have been born in Fishkill, New York, which is south of Wappinger Falls, the year Steven Spielberg made the movie *Jaws*.

"Whoa! This is just too way cool for words! Lock up your pets and children! The Frankenfish are coming! Fabulous! Fabulous! Fabulous!" Bryan DePalma, whose birth name was Francis Finister, could not contain his glee. "I've spent a lot of time at Placid Pond filming the bullfrogs. I was thinking of something like *Creature From the Black Lagoon*—the old black and white movie classic made back in 1954 starring Ben Chapman as Gillman. But bullfrogs aren't all that scary, know what I mean? A good creature feature requires a creature with teeth. Man, I hope those fish get big enough to be really scary on film."

Bryan DePalma's Alibi: "I don't know when the bullfrogs started disappearing. I missed a lot of filming time at the pond because Brian DePalma's lawyers keep sending me letters threatening me with a lawsuit if I don't remove my name from my own films. Hey, the way I figure it, this a free country and I have a right to call myself anything I want, and it's not like I spelled my name exactly like that DePalma director dude's, so what's the problem here?"

The Solution

Blake Fishman had a problem. His father brought an electric eel back from his business trip, but Blake's mother won't let him have more than one aquarium. Blake knew he couldn't put his beautiful new pet into the same tank with his old pets, so he let his old pets go. He knew they'd find something to eat in Placid Pond, but he misjudged how much they'd eat. When he realized that he had unwittingly caused an eco-crisis in Placid Pond he tried to catch the northern snakeheads, but he was not successful.

Information About the Suspects

Suspect 1—Robert "Bull" Butman

- Fish Creek, Wisconsin, is between Egg Harbor and Sister Bay, Wisconsin.

- *Don't Go Near the Water* by William Brinkley was published in 1956.

- *Rana catesbeiana,* the North American bullfrog, has legs that are almost 10 inches long. The males emit a loud, booming jug-a-rum call on summer nights.

Suspect 2—Long Yu Tang

- Whitefish, Montana, is between Lupfer and Halfmoon, Montana.

- Laurence Fishburne was born in 1961.

- Chinese New Year is celebrated on the first day of the first moon on the Chinese lunar calendar, so it falls somewhere between January 21 and February 19.

- Northern snakeheads are delicious, and in the Asian culture their flesh is believed to have curative powers.

Suspect 3—Blake Fishman

- Spearfish, South Dakota, is northwest, not south, of Crook City, South Dakota.

- Izaak Walton died in 1683.

- The *Electrophorus electricus,* the electric eel, comes from South America. It produces a pulse of low-level energy that helps it detect nearby objects, but it can also produce 450 to 600 volts of electricity—enough to kill prey.

- Mauritania is located on the northwestern coast of the African continent.

Suspect 4—Bryan DePalma

- Fishkill, New York, is south of Wappinger Falls, New York.

- Steven Spielberg made the movie *Jaws* in 1975.

- *Creature From the Black Lagoon,* a black-and-white movie made in 1954, starred Ben Chapman as Gillman.

- Brian DePalma is a film director.

The Mystery of the Fiery Facial

The Crime

Miss Quaildart, teacher of Bay Ridge High School's Advanced Health and Beauty class, planned a special treat for the day before the senior prom—the girls in her class would learn how to give facials. Which girl would be the recipient of the class facial? Miss Quaildart might not have known whom she was going to choose, but the girls in the class did. Brittany would get the facial. Brittany always got what she wanted. But this time Brittany got more than she expected. The facial cream had barely touched her skin before she started screaming. Miss Quaildart moved quickly, submerging Brittany's face in a pan of water and scrubbing the cream off, but she didn't move quickly enough. Brittany's peaches and cream complexion was more like a tomatoes and boiled lobster complexion by the time class ended. Lab tests have revealed the presence of capsaicin in the facial cream.

The Question

Who sabotaged the facial?

The Suspects

Suspect 1—Bambi Doe

Bambi Doe, a student in Miss Quaildart's class, claims to have been born in Loveland, Ohio, which is north of Twenty Mile Stand, the year that Helen Louise Leonard was born.

"Brittany was my friend until she stole my boyfriend, Buck," Bambi told us. "Then she dropped him and he came crawling back to me, but I said, 'No way!' Anyway, I don't need a boyfriend right now. I'm concentrating on my modeling career. Someday I'm going to be a bigger super-model than Iman Mohamed Abdulmajid was. She is totally amazing! She was born in a poor village in Nigeria to the village healer and one of his six wives. Then she came here, I guess as an exchange student, and got discovered, and then she got rich, and then she went back to her own country to run a medical clinic for children. I want to be just like her, except for, maybe, running a medical clinic because there's enough of those here already and I don't think I'd be good around kids who are throwing up and stuff."

Bambi Doe's Alibi: "I was there. Actually, I'm the one who spread the cream on Brittany's face. I was wearing latex gloves because my hands are sensitive to chemicals and you never know what's going to be in the bargain-basement supplies Miss Quaildart orders, what with the measly budget the school board gives the Health and Beauty program. So, anyway, she started to scream and I couldn't figure out what was wrong so I kept putting the cream on her face, which I guess wasn't such a good idea. Then Miss Quaildart shoved me aside, really kind of rudely, and pushed Brittany's head into the sink. Buck should have seen her then." Bambi smiled. "She looked like a drowned pomeranian with a bad henna job."

Suspect 2—Barbie Ann Kent

Barbie Ann Kent, a student in Miss Quaildart's class, claims to have been born in Loveville, Maryland, which is between the towns of Hollywood and California, the year that Sophia Villani Acicolone was born.

"Want to see my Barbie doll collection?" Barbie Ann Kent led us into a bedroom lined with shelves of stunningly dressed dolls. "I get Barbie dolls for Christmas and my birthday and just whenever. Actually, it's getting kind of boring now, but my mother thinks it's cute so I keep on getting them. The doll was invented by a woman named Ruth Handler way back in history, you know, like 1965, something like that, and she named it after her mother, who I guess was named Barbie, or maybe Barbara, 'cause mothers aren't usually named something like Barbie. Anyway, she sent it around to all the toy companies and Mattel finally took a chance on it because they were looking for a doll that would teach girls about going out into the real world and getting real jobs like, you know, fashion model and actress and debutante and people who live in Malibu, and things like that."

"Brittany used to like my doll collection," Barbie told us. "Or she pretended to. She came over here almost every day until she managed to steal my boyfriend, Joe. He's in the army now."

Barbie Ann Kent's Alibi: "Oh, sure, I was right there when it happened. I was holding the jar of facial cream while Bambi spread it on Brittany's face. You know, it looked kind of funny, like it had little red flecks in it, but a lot of the things in Miss Quaildart's room look kind of funny, so I didn't think anything of it."

Suspect 3—Brandi Whine

Brandi Whine, a student in Miss Quaildart's class, claims to have been born in Love Valley, North Carolina, which is between Windy Gap and Old Gilreath, the year that Margarita Carmen Cansino was born.

"Come on up!" Brandi Whine led us to a bedroom that was papered with movie posters. "I'm going to be a famous actress someday," she informed us with utter confidence. "Just like one of the Barrymores. Drew is the only one I've ever heard of, but my mother told me there were others, like her parents, Ethel and John Wilson Barrymore. But you know who I absolutely adore? George Peppard, that sexy old guy who starred in *The Great Waldo Pepper*. He was so cute!"

"Did I have a reason not to like Brittany?" Brandi laughed. "Yeah, like, welcome to the whole world. She stole my boyfriend, Brandon. She steals everybody's boyfriend. It's her hobby. Brandon kind of wants me to take him back," she confided. "He was going to take me to a matinee earlier this week but I got detention and had to work it off in Miss Quaildart's room, helping her clean up after the slobs in Beginning Health and Beauty."

Brandi Whine's Alibi: "I was in the room, but I was in the back of the group so I didn't get a good look at what happened."

Suspect 4—Buffy DeCar

Buffy DeCar, a student in Miss Quaildart's class, claims to have been born in Lovejoy, Georgia, which is north of Flippen, the year that Florence Nightingale Graham was born.

We found Buffy behind the counter of her family's store, The Hot Spot, which is devoted to all forms of chili products. "I was stuck working here instead of going to the prom. Do you want to know why?" Buffy asked bitterly. "Brittany stole my date, Beau. I hope he enjoyed looking at her blistered face all night."

"Working here isn't all that bad," Buffy finally admitted with a shrug. "It's quiet most of the time, which gives me a chance to study things like botany and chemistry, which are going to be useful when I develop my own cosmetic products. I'm thinking about basing a line of skin products on fruits. I've managed to make an astringent distillation from smallage, which is a variety of small grapefruit, and I've mixed it with essential oils from the lovage plant, which has a wonderful mint aroma. The lovage plant even has little heart-shaped leaves that are going to look adorable on the label. My mom said I can sell my line of Lovage Lotions in the store once I get them developed and packaged."

Buffy DeCar's Alibi: "I wasn't even in class that day. I was so upset about Brittany and Beau I stayed home with a migraine."

The Solution

Brittany's fiery facial was a group effort. Buffy obtained capsaicin in the form of a hot chili pepper from her parents' store. She crushed it and gave it to Brandi, who mixed it into the jar of facial cream while she was serving her detention in Miss Quaildart's room. Barbie held the jar while Bambi, being careful to wear gloves to protect her sensitive hands, smeared the cream onto Brittany's face. All four of the girls had lost boyfriends to their classmate. They obviously decided that revenge is best served hot.

Information About the Suspects

Suspect 1—Bambi Doe

- Loveland, Ohio, is south, not north, of Twenty Mile Stand, Ohio.

- Helen Louise Leonard, better known as Lillian Russell, was born in 1861.

- Iman Mohamed Abdulmajid was born in Mogadishu, Somalia. Her mother was a gynecologist. Her father was a diplomat.

- After a successful modeling career, Iman became a successful business executive with her own line of cosmetics. She has been married to rock star David Bowie since 1992.

Suspect 2—Barbie Ann Kent

- Loveville, Maryland, is not between Hollywood and California, Maryland. It is northwest of both towns.

- Sophia Villani Acicolone, better known as Sophia Loren, was born in 1934.

- The Barbie doll was invented in 1959 by Ruth Handler, whose husband was the cofounder of Mattel. She named the doll after her daughter Barbara. The doll was intended to be a fashion doll for teenagers.

Suspect 3—Brandi Whine

- Love Valley, North Carolina, is not between Windy Gap and Old Gilreath. It is south of both towns.

- Margarita Carmen Cansino, better known as Rita Hayworth, was born in 1918.

- Drew Barrymore is the daughter of John Drew Barrymore and Ildiko Jaid. George Peppard was not in *The Great Waldo Pepper*. Robert Redford was.

Suspect 4—Buffy DeCar

- Lovejoy, Georgia, is southwest, not north, of Flippen, Georgia.

- Florence Nightingale Graham, better known as Elizabeth Arden, was born in 1878.

- Smallage is a wild form of celery.

- Lovage leaves are not heart-shaped. They look like celery.

The Mystery of the Pilfered Peacocks

The Crime

Millionaire Sylvia Swanson loved her summer cottage overlooking Butterfly Lake. She had always loved the view from her balcony on cool, clear mornings—the purple-hued mountains in the distance, a ghostly mist rising from the mirrored surface of the lake, the peacocks strutting on the emerald green lawn. It took Sylvia several cups of morning café latte to realize that this morning's scene contained no peacocks. It took the ser-vants several minutes to remember that they hadn't seen any peacocks on the lawn in the past week. It took the garden-er several hours to ascertain that there were no peacocks on the estate at all.

The Question

What happened to Sylvia Swanson's peacocks?

The Suspects

Suspect 1—Clothilde Cloche

Clothilde Cloche, a local milliner, claims to have been born in Swanville, Maine, which is southwest of Bucksport, the year that *Summer of the Swans* won the Newbery Medal.

"Sylvia Swanson's birds have flown their coop, eh?" Clothilde Cloche remarked with some amusement. "Well, I'm sure that she'll get more. That woman is loaded. And stingy. She orders hats from me from time to time, and she always complains about the price. I have pointed out that it costs a lot of money to do the extravagant feathery creations she likes. She likes aigrettes, especially from the Ardeidae family. That's the egret family," Clothilde Cloche explained. "The snowy egret was hunted almost to extinction for its plumage and now it is a protected bird. But Sylvia Swanson doesn't seem to understand that. She wants what she wants and she thinks she should be able to have it."

Clothilde Cloche's Alibi: "Yes, I use peacock feathers in my hats. I bought those over there on my work table from Gail Greene, Flora Fowler and Tiny Tooch. I didn't ask where they got them. I don't care. That doesn't make me a thief."

Suspect 2—Gail Greene

Gail Greene, Sylvia Swanson's gardener, claims to have been born in Duck, West Virginia, which is north of Dingy, the year that *Mother Carey's Chickens* by Kate Douglas Wiggins was published.

"The peacocks!" Gail Greene rolled her eyes in exasperation. "It was hard enough to do the gardening exactly the way Mrs. Swanson wants it done without having to work around those nasty, ill-tempered birds. Every time I leaned over to deadhead the perennial border one of them would nip me in the buttocks. It's a relief to have them gone."

"Oh, don't get me wrong," Gail hastened to add. "I like birds. I even own a pair of Carolina parakeets. They're small green birds with long tails and green and yellow heads—pretty little things. They're originally from South America, just like the peacocks. But they're a lot nicer than peacocks."

Gail Greene's Alibi: "I'm a gardener, not a bird babysitter," Gail Greene said defensively. "How should I know where the peacocks went? Where did I get the feathers I sold to Clothilde Cloche? I was always picking them up from the lawn where those darn birds dropped them."

Suspect 3—Flora Fowler

Flora Fowler, owner of Pheasant Farm Frozen Pheasant Company, claims to have been born in Crow Agency, Montana, "out in the middle of nowhere on Route 82," the year that ornithologist William Bartram died.

"We've been very successful the past few years," Flora Fowler explained as she led us through the short row of pheasant coops to the abattoir and processing sheds beyond. "You'd be amazed at how many families want an alternative to turkey for the holidays, and that alternative is a Pheasant Farm Frozen Pheasant, shipped with a prepared wild-rice stuffing and old-fashioned southern yams. We used to raise all of the pheasants ourselves, but Her Royal Highness objected to the noise of our birds." Flora Fowler nodded in the direction of the Swanson mansion. "So we've had to close down most of our coops and bring in the majority of our birds from elsewhere. Pheasants aren't always easy to find. We always have more orders than we can fill."

"You know what the irony is? Swanson's lawyers told the zoning board that my pheasants are obnoxious, filthy birds unfit to be raised near a private residence, then she bought a dozen peacocks for her lawn. You know what peacocks are? They're pheasants with an exaggerated ego! The common peacock, *Cathartes aura,* and the Javanese peacock, *Struthio camelus,* are both members of the family Phasianidae—just like pheasants!"

Flora Fowler's Alibi: "Oh, give me a break! Tell that Swanson witch to leave me alone! She's already done me enough harm. Where did I get the feathers I sold to Clothilde?" Flora's eyes narrowed. "I picked them up off Swanson's lawn. Why shouldn't I make a few extra bucks when I can? It's not like she was going to use them."

Suspect 4—Tina "Tiny" Tooch

Tina "Tiny" Tooch, owner of Butterfly Lake Diet Spa and Spiritual Self-Actualization Center, claims to have been born in Goose Creek, South Carolina, which is west of Charity, the year that *How to Succeed in Business Without Really Trying* won the Pulitzer Prize for Drama.

"Breathe and move, breathe and move ..." Tiny Tooch, dressed in a flowing lavender caftan, flapped her arms like a butterfly as she led us through the spa's meditation garden. "Feel yourself become as light as mist. Visualize! Visualize! Visualize something more pleasant than peacocks," she said when we asked her about the missing birds. "They used to wander over here from the estate, probably because no one remembered to feed them. They're ill-tempered birds at the best of times, but they were hungry, and my clients were hungry. That's not a good combination. A little more than a week ago, one of the birds snatched a cucumber toast from Mrs. Abernathy's chubby fingers and Mrs. Abernathy went after it. A few other clients thought that she was trying to catch it so the spa's chef could cook it, and they joined in the chase. My dear, it was bedlam!"

"Move like a bird!" Tiny Tooch changed the subject suddenly. Her arms at her sides, she glided down the path toward a group of women painting watercolor still lifes of food. "Move like a *Cygnus buccinator.* You may be large, but you are beautiful! Raise your voice to the sky like the trumpet for which you are named. You may be related to ducks and geese, but you are better than that! Move like the aquatic queen you are!"

Tina "Tiny" Tooch's Alibi: "I was here, and everywhere, as we all are, all the time," Tiny answered. "Oh, you're serious." Her demeanor changed. "I don't know where I was when the pesky things went missing, but I wouldn't have taken them. Do you know why?" She lowered her voice so she wouldn't be overheard by her clients. "My cardinal rule of business is 'Never Upset a Wealthy Woman.' The feathers I sold to Clothilde? Those were from the Abernathy incident. What else was I going to do with them?"

The Solution

Gail Greene was tired of being nipped in the buttocks by ill-tempered birds, and Flora Fowler was always happy to have more members of the Phasianidae family for her frozen pheasant business. It was a partnership made in heaven for everyone but the peacocks.

Information About the Suspects

Suspect 1—Clothilde Cloche

- Swanville, Maine, is southwest of Bucksport, Maine.

- *Summer of the Swans* won the Newbery Medal in 1971.

- Aigrettes, feathers from egrets and herons, are used in hat-making.

- The snowy egret, a member of the family Ardeidae, was hunted almost to extinction for its plumage and now is a protected bird.

Suspect 2—Gail Greene

- Duck, West Virginia, is south, not north, of Dingy, West Virginia.

- *Mother Carey's Chickens* by Kate Douglas Wiggins was published in 1911.

- Carolina parakeets were small green birds with long tails and yellow heads with orange or scarlet cheeks and foreheads. They are extinct. The last one was seen in south Florida in the early 1900s.

- Peacocks originated in India and Ceylon.

Suspect 3—Flora Fowler

- Crow Agency, Montana, may be "out in the middle of nowhere," but it's on Route 90, not Route 82.

- Ornithologist William Bartram died in 1823.

- Pheasants and peacocks both belong to the family Phasianidae, but the common peacock is *Pavo cristatus*, and the Javanese peacock is *Pavo muticus*. *Cathartes aura* is the turkey vulture, and *Struthio camelus* is the ostrich.

Suspect 4—Tina "Tiny" Tooch

- Goose Creek, South Carolina, is west of Charity, South Carolina.

- *How to Succeed in Business Without Really Trying* won the Pulitzer Prize for Drama in 1962.

- *Cygnus buccinator*, the trumpeter swan, is named for its resonant call.

- Swans are related to ducks and geese.

The Mystery of the Runaway Reptiles

The Crime

Professor Orville Ophidian, noted herpetologist, was upset. When he returned from his daily walk he found that his pet serpent was missing from its cage. But his reaction was understated compared to that of his wife. "It's gone?" she screamed hysterically. "Where gone? Out there in the desert gone or in here under the couch gone? There is a rattlesnake loose in this house? Is that what you're telling me? I hate your snakes! I've always hated your snakes! And now one of them is loose! I'm out of here!" she screamed. "You'll be hearing from my lawyer, Orville! This is mental abuse. Don't expect to get out of this marriage cheap!"

The Question

What happened to Professor Ophidian's snake?

The Suspects

Suspect 1—Lucy Loveless Ophidian

Lucy Loveless Ophidian, Professor Ophidian's wife, claims to have been born in Snake Hill, New York, which is northeast of Round Lake, the year that Bill Haley & His Comets released "Shake, Rattle & Roll."

"Do you know what it's like to feel frightened in your own home?" Lucy Ophidian snapped as she turned down the volume of the television in her motel room. "That snake had me so unnerved I could barely concentrate on the book I'm writing. It's about the Borden murders and their hold on the popular imagination, even now, more than 100 years later. I'm sure you've heard the rhyme, 'Lizzie Borden took an ax and gave her mother forty whacks. And when she saw what she had done, she gave her father forty-one.' That's not strictly true, of course. Lizzie was acquitted of Abby and Andrew Borden's murders. But you can understand why the facts permuted. 'Lizzie Borden, or maybe someone else, took an ax and gave her stepmother between seventeen and nineteen whacks. And when she saw what she had done, she gave her father between nine and eleven whacks.' Isn't as catchy, is it?"

Lucy Loveless Ophidian's Alibi: "I was watching *Court TV* in my bedroom. I heard doors opening and closing in the house, and cars coming and going in the driveway, but I didn't pay any attention. I was particularly fascinated by a lawsuit concerning ownership of a Persian cat after a divorce settlement. There is no chance I will petition for ownership of any of the creatures in our house," Lucy Ophidian added with a shudder. "They're all snakes and the mice that Orville raises to feed the reptiles. They're disgusting."

Suspect 2—Chuck Waggoner

Chuck Waggoner, a friend of Orville and Lucy Ophidian, claims to have been born in Chili, Wisconsin, northeast of Veefkind, the year that Harriet Mulford Lothrop's *The Five Little Peppers and How They Grew* was published.

"Howdy!" Chuck Waggoner greeted us at the door of his incredibly messy trailer. "Hey, excuse all the pots and pans and dishes everywhere. I'm developing a new recipe for an upcoming chili contest in Baja California Sur, which is in the mountains west of California's Big Sur. It's not that hard to make a good chili," Chuck Waggoner informed us. "There are thousands of variations. But the Baja California Sur Cookoff is the toughest competition in the United States. To win it, a chili has to be hot and savory, but it also needs what I call 'the X factor.' It needs some interesting taste that the judges can't quite name. I tried chocolate last year but it turns out that isn't so unusual in chili. I'm working up a recipe with a sweet, mild pepper called *Allium sativum* and a much spicier chili called the *Allium sepa*. And the 'X factor,' of course."

Chuck Waggoner's Alibi: "I was right here in my trailer, stewing lizard meat. It was interesting. Sort of like chicken but with more legs. I'm used to catching all kinds of stuff out in the desert. I've been doing it ever since I was a boy."

Suspect 3—Sidney "Sidewinder Sid" Smythe

"Sidewinder Sid" Smythe claims to have been born in Snake Creek, South Dakota, which is between Little Eagle and Mobridge, the year that Charley Pride released his first hit song, "Snakes Crawl by Night."

"It's been a bad year for snakes," Sidewinder Sid Smythe told us. "That's how I make my living—catching snakes for sale to zoos, venom milkers and private collectors. I'm the one who caught the sidewinder Professor Orville has. Used to have," Smythe corrected himself. "It might not have gone far. The *Crotalus cerastes* tends to burrow into the sand during the hottest part of the day. I'll make a point of swinging by his property toward evening, when the snake might be more active."

"I heard that the missus got totally freaked out." Smythe chuckled. "Sidewinders aren't worth getting that worked up about. Now, *Crotalus atrox,* that's another story. If the professor's missing snake were a western diamond-back, I'd say, 'Run for the hills, Lucy!' Those snakes bite more people in the United States every year than any other venomous snake."

Sidney "Sidewinder Sid" Smythe's Alibi: "I was out beating the bushes, quite literally, trying to figure out how I was going to make the payments on my new truck. If I don't find some snakes soon, I'm going to be in serious financial straits."

Suspect 4—Chandler Chick

Chandler Chick, Professor Ophidian's neighbor, claims to have been born in Snaketown, Arizona, which is southwest of Sun Lakes, the year that Steve "Stone Cold" Austin, also known as "The Texas Rattlesnake," was born.

"It is absolutely unconscionable to keep a poisonous snake in a house. Look what's happened now! It's loose, and my babies are in danger." Chandler Chick led us to a coop in his backyard around which a dozen hens scratched in the dusty earth. "I have mostly Rhode Island Reds, a breed developed in New England to be a good, reliable egg producer. But these are my babies." Chandler Chick pointed to a pair of dust mops with combs and wattles. "Cochins," he explained. "These are the fowl I exhibit at the state fair. They lay only a few eggs a week. They aren't bad to eat, although they aren't as plump as they look. They're just adorable, big balls of plumage, aren't you, my plucky little pullet pets?"

"I've lost chickens ever since the professor got that snake," Chandler Chick said angrily. "I told him I thought it was getting out, but he wouldn't believe me. Well, now he can't deny that it gets out. If it comes slithering over here looking for another chicken dinner I'll be ready, with my gun."

Chandler Chick's Alibi: "I was at my computer researching ways to protect a chicken coop from predators. I heard a car door slam in the Ophidian's driveway, but I didn't go to the window to take a look. I figured it was Lucy Ophidian storming off after one of their ferocious fights."

The Solution

Lucy Ophidian and Chandler Chick do not have to worry about the wandering sidewinder. Nor should Sidewinder Sid Smythe waste much time around the Ophidian home looking for a way to earn enough money to make a car payment. Professor Ophidian's rattlesnake has been transformed into the X factor in Chuck Waggoner's secret chili recipe. Chuck claims that he has had practice in catching things out in the desert, and according to Sidewinder Sid, the *Crotalus cerastes* "isn't worth getting all worked up about." In addition to a few packages of "X factor," a search of Chuck Waggoner's freezer might also turn up one of Chandler Chick's missing chickens.

Information About the Suspects

Suspect 1—Lucy Loveless Ophidian

- Snake Hill, New York, is northeast of Round Lake, New York.

- Bill Haley & His Comets released "Shake, Rattle & Roll" in 1954.

- The Borden murders occurred in 1892.

- Lizzie Borden was acquitted of Abby and Andrew Borden's murders. The number of ax blows differs according to the sources used, but both victims had fewer blows than the popular rhyme. Abby Borden suffered from 17 to 19 blows, and Andrew Borden suffered from 9 to 11 blows.

Suspect 2—Chuck Waggoner

- Chili, Wisconsin, is south, not northeast, of Veefkind, Wisconsin.

- Harriet Mulford Lothrop's *The Five Little Peppers and How They Grew* was published in 1881.

- Baja California Sur is the southern portion of the Baja California peninsula, which is part of Mexico.

- California's Big Sur is located farther north, along the central part of California's coastline. Mountains west of Big Sur would be in the Pacific Ocean.

- *Allium sativum* is garlic, not a variety of pepper.

- *Allium sepa* is onion, not a variety of pepper.

Suspect 3—Sidney "Sidewinder Sid" Smythe

- Snake Creek, South Dakota, is located between Little Eagle and Mobridge, South Dakota.

- Charley Pride released his first hit song, "Snakes Crawl by Night" in 1966.

- The sidewinder rattlesnake, the *Crotalus cerastes,* tends to burrow into the sand during the hottest part of the day and be more active in the evening.

- *Crotalus atrox,* the western diamondback, bites more people in the United States every year than any other venomous snake.

Suspect 4—Chandler Chick

- Snaketown, Arizona, is southwest of Sun Lakes, Arizona.

- Steve "Stone Cold" Austin, also known as "The Texas Rattlesnake," was born in 1964.

- The Rhode Island Red breed of chicken was developed in the New England states of Massachusetts and Rhode Island. It is a reliable egg producer.

- The Cochin breed of chicken is primarily ornamental and is used for exhibitions. It is not a good egg producer. Cochins have an abundance of feathers.

The Mystery of the Superfluous Sevens

The Crime

The lottery number that Septima Sevenridge has played for years—seven 7's—finally was a winner. Septima cut short a seven-day trip to Atlantic City with her card club, the Lucky Sevens, in order to rush home and claim her $700,000 in winnings. Alas, the lottery ticket she had affixed to her refrigerator with a red magnet in the shape of a seven was gone.

The Question

Who stole Septima Sevenridge's lottery ticket?

The Suspects

Suspect 1—Yedi Onyedi

Yedi Onyedi, the manager of the 7-Eleven where Septima Sevenridge bought her ticket, claims to have been born in Seven Corners, Virginia, which is west of Washington, D.C., the year that Ingmar Bergman made the movie *The Seventh Seal.*

"Septima Sevenridge was a pain in the neck," Yedi Onyedi said uncharitably. "She insisted that the seven 7s lottery number was hers and hers alone, as if she invented it. If she came in here half an hour before the lottery drawing and found I'd sold the number to someone else, she'd pitch a fit. So I figured, fine, I'll print out a ticket for her and keep it in my drawer until she comes in for it, but a couple of times she didn't come in until after the drawing and she refused to pay for a ticket she knew was a loser, so I had to pay for the ticket myself. She didn't see anything wrong with that."

"This is a boring job," Yedi Onyedi confided. "I pass my time in here doing things like trying to figure out which of my customers match up with the Seven Deadly Sins. There's Pride, Greed, Lust, Envy, Gluttony, Anger and Sloth. I don't quite have Mrs. Sevenridge figured, but I know which of the Seven Deadly Sins I'm falling for when she's in here. Anger. Sometimes I want to put my hands on that bony little neck of hers ... But I don't! Nope! It's not nice to kill the customers. I know that!"

Yedi Onyedi's Alibi: "Oh, man, like I could actually get away from this store long enough to break into her house looking for a lottery ticket. That's a dream."

Suspect 2—Zeeve Seuven

Zeeve Seuven, a regular customer of the 7-Eleven, claims to have been born in Seven Springs, North Carolina, which is east of Bucklesberry, the year that Annika Hansen was born to Magnus and Erin Hansen.

"That lottery ticket should have been mine," Zeeve Seuven informed us adamantly. "Seven is my lucky number. But Yedi won't sell me the seven 7s ticket because he doesn't want that old biddy nagging at him when she finds out someone else has it. It isn't fair that she won $700,000 on a ticket that should have been mine."

Zeeve Seuven's Alibi: "I was at home watching a video about the Seven Wonders of the Ancient World. Do you want me to name them for you? There's the Sphinx of Gaza, the Hanging Gardens of Babylon, the Great Wall of China, King Tutankhamun's tomb, the Acropolis in Athens, the Colosseum in Rome and the temple at Macchu Pichu."

Suspect 3—Settanta Settecento

Settanta Settecento, Septima Sevenridge's neighbor, claims to have been born in Seven Fields, Pennsylvania, which is east of Knob, the year that *Seventh Heaven,* the movie for which Janet Gaynor won the Academy Award for Best Actress, was released.

"All right, I was in her house. I admit it!" Settanta Settecento snapped. "I promised to feed her cat, 7-Up, while she was away gambling like some kind of young floozy.

7-Up is her cat's name, not what I fed it. I fed it cat food. The cheap cat food. I'm surprised that cat hasn't run away. And I left the door unlocked, so sue me! I'm an old woman. What do you expect from me? Let her hire someone to feed the cat the next time she goes away!"

Settanta Settecento's Alibi: "I went into her house. I fed the cat. I went home and watched *Snow White and the Seven Dwarfs* with my great-grandchildren. They wanted to watch *Seven*, the movie with Morgan Freeman and Brad Pitt, but I said, 'No, we're going to watch this movie Walt Disney made when I was 10 years old.' They thought it was dumb. I said, 'I don't care. Sit down. When you're as famous as Walt Disney you can watch anything you want.'"

Suspect 4—Shichi Ichi

Shichi Ichi, Septima Sevenridge's mailman, claims to have been born in Seventh Day Hollow, New York, which is northeast of Hydeville, the year that the movie *Seven Brides for Seven Brothers* was released.

"The door wasn't just unlocked, it was open," Shichi Ichi told us. "I went in and looked around because I thought something might have happened to Mrs. Sevenridge. It happens with old people. You notice their mail hasn't been picked up for a few days, you knock on the door and there's no answer, what are you supposed to do? Just walk away? Fortunately, I didn't find her body in the house."

Shichi Ichi's Alibi: "I was running late because I stopped to watch *Seven Samurai* with one of my postal customers," Shichi Ichi admitted. "I'm sure you know the one—the 1954 black-and-white film directed by Akira Kurosawa. I'm a sucker for that movie. The story, which is set in sixteenth-century Japan, is about a village that hires seven samurai to defend it against bandits. It's a long movie, but it's full of great characters. Anyway, when I finally got to Mrs. Sevenridge's house, I found the door wide open. There was no dead body in the house, but there was a red magnet in the shape of a seven on the floor. I remember picking it up and putting it back on the refrigerator. Can I go now? I have mail to deliver."

The Solution

Zeeve Seuven was so angry that Septima Sevenridge won $700,000 with a number he felt he should have been allowed to play that he went to her house. Maybe he wanted to confront her, or maybe he knew she was away and he planned to break in to steal the ticket. It must have come as a pleasant surprise to find the door unlocked and the lottery ticket on the refrigerator. He snatched it quickly, knocking the 7-shaped magnet to the floor, and left. Since then he's been trying to figure out how to cash in the lottery ticket without revealing that he was the one who took it.

Information About the Suspects

Suspect 1—Yedi Onyedi

- Seven Corners, Virginia, is west of Washington, D.C.

- Ingmar Bergman made the movie *The Seventh Seal* in 1957.

- The Seven Deadly Sins are Pride, Greed, Lust, Envy, Gluttony, Anger and Sloth.

Suspect 2—Zeeve Seuven

- Seven Springs, North Carolina, is west, not east, of Bucklesberry, North Carolina.

- The fictional character Annika Hansen, also known as Seven of Nine on the *Star Trek: Voyager* television series, was born in 2348, or stardate 25479.

- The Seven Wonders of the Ancient World are the Statue of Zeus at Olympia, the Colossus of Rhodes, the Great Pyramid at Giza, the Hanging Gardens of Babylon, the Mausoleum at Helicarnassus, the Temple of Artemis at Ephesus and the Lighthouse at Alexandria.

Suspect 3—Settanta Settecento

- Seven Fields, Pennsylvania, is east of Knob, Pennsylvania.

- *Seventh Heaven* was released in 1927. In 1928 Janet Gaynor won the Academy Award for Best Actress for her performances in that movie, as well as for her roles in *Street Angel* and *Sunrise*.

- *Snow White and the Seven Dwarfs* was made by Walt Disney and his animators in 1937.

- The movie *Seven* stars Morgan Freeman and Brad Pitt.

Suspect 4—Shichi Ichi

- Seventh Day Hollow, New York, is northeast of Hydeville, New York.

- *Seven Brides for Seven Brothers* was released in 1954.

- *Seven Samurai*, a 1954 black-and-white film directed by Akira Kurosawa, tells the story of a sixteenth-century Japanese village that hired seven samurai to defend it against bandit raids. The movie is three and a half hours long.

The Mystery of the Sullied Signs

The Crime

"HI. VOTE FOR ME." The orange and yellow signs were ubiquitous in Pleasant Valley. So were Hiram "Hi" Falutin and his promises. If he were elected mayor he would eliminate fees for dog licenses, hold a barbecue at the Town Hall every Fourth of July and give a Christmas gift to every child in the Pleasant Valley schools. He would pay for his proposed improvements to town government with the proceeds from a gigantic festival that would put Pleasant Valley on the map. The details of the festival were vague, but they were alarming enough to encourage three other Pleasant Valley residents to oppose Hiram Falutin in the mayoral election.

Two days before Election Day a vandal struck. All of Hiram Falutin's signs were changed to read "HI: NOT FOR ME."

The Question

Who vandalized Hiram Falutin's campaign signs?

The Suspects

Suspect 1—Hiram "Hi" Falutin

Hiram Falutin, candidate for mayor, claims to have been born in Jubilee, North Carolina, which is north of Churchland, the year that Phineas Taylor Barnum died.

"You know why the other candidates hate me?" Hiram Falutin asked. "I am a man of vision. I want the best for Pleasant Valley. I want to put this town on the map. Pleasant Valley means America and America means something, that's my motto. Now, you take all that park land that lies outside of town, that's just going to waste. What do you have there? Trees! Grass! Squirrels! Nothing! I envision an enormous arena where we could hold an American version of La Tomatina, the festival they've held over there in Zaragoza, Spain, ever since the Middle Ages. Basically, it's a big jousting tournament, with horses and knights in armor and ladies waving those pretty little handkerchiefs. What could be more American than that?"

Hiram Falutin's Alibi: "Who needs an alibi when you have what it takes to make this town a great place to be from?" Hiram Falutin asked rhetorically. "I think this act of vandalism will only serve to show the residents of Pleasant Valley just what kind of people are running against me and the lengths to which they will go to prevent me from bringing my vision to the people of this great American town."

Suspect 2—Mary Onette

Mary Onette, candidate for mayor of Pleasant Valley, claims to have been born in Jubilee, Indiana, which is between Raymar and Hamerville, the year that *The Greatest Show on Earth* won the Academy Award for Best Motion Picture.

"I have heard rumors about Hiram's plans for this town," Mary Onette said wearily. "He's such an idiot. He has no idea how easily things can get out of hand. Consider Bread & Puppet's Domestic Resurrection Circus. Bread & Puppet had put on the annual event for 27 years. In the beginning, a few thousand people showed up. Then 20,000 people attended. Then 40,000 people. Then, even more. Some of them came with alcohol, then others came with drugs. Eventually someone died in a fight, and the director of Bread & Puppet put an end to the annual Domestic Resurrection Circus. Hiram is a fool if he thinks failing to attract people to our town is a problem. The possibility that his festival would attract as many people to our town as Bread & Puppet's Domestic Resurrection Circus attracted to Glover, Vermont, is the scenario that terrifies me."

Mary Onette's Alibi: "My niece and two young nephews were visiting me that week, so I spent a lot of time baking chocolate chip cookies, watching videos and helping them draw pictures with colored markers."

Suspect 3—E. (Ellen) Quel-Wright

E. Quel-Wright, feminist candidate for mayor of Pleasant Valley, claims to have been born in Celebration, Florida, which is west of Kissimmee, the year that Samuel Goldfish died.

"Don't get me started on the subject of Hiram Falutin!" E. Quel-Wright warned.

"The man's a chauvinist pig! Do you know what his plans for the Big Festival are? Well, I don't actually know, either, but I've heard rumors that he wants to develop a Wife Carrying World Championship. Believe it or not, there already is a Wife Carrying World Championship every year in Finland, but Falutin thinks that's too far for Americans to travel to compete for the top prize, which, by the way, is the wife's weight in beer."

E. Quel-Wright's Alibi: "I didn't have time to destroy Falutin's campaign signs because I was out running a real campaign based on real issues, not some cockamamie idea based on the wife-stealing proclivities of nineteenth-century Finnish thieves."

Suspect 4—George Gathering Crowd

George Gathering Crowd, candidate for mayor of Pleasant Valley, claims to have been born in Jubilee, Pennsylvania, which is east of Tooley Corners, the year that Jim Thorpe's Olympic medals were posthumously restored.

"I decided to run for mayor when I was told that Hiram Falutin's proposed festival would be an imitation of the Gathering of Nations Powwow that is held every April in Albuquerque, New Mexico," George Gathering Crowd told us. "Members of more than 500 tribes from all over the United States and Canada gather to dance, sell their crafts and crown Miss Indian World. Holding a cheapened version here in Pleasant Valley would demean an important Native American tradition and make a laughingstock of this town."

"Hiram Falutin is the kind of man who greets Native Americans by holding up his hand and saying 'How.' He's an ignorant fool," George Gathering Crowd said curtly. "He cannot be elected mayor of Pleasant Valley. Even the dogs in this town deserve better than that."

George Gathering Crowd's Alibi: "I was in Pleasant Valley Park imagining what this land must have been like before the arrival of Hiram Falutin's ancestors."

The Solution

Hiram Falutin defaced his own campaign signs hoping to cast doubt on the integrity of the other candidates and win sympathy for his own campaign.

Information About the Suspects

Suspect 1—Hiram "Hi" Falutin

- Jubilee, North Carolina, is southwest, not north, of Churchland, North Carolina.

- Phineas Taylor Barnum died in 1891.

- La Tomatina is held in Bunol, Spain, not Zaragoza, Spain. It reportedly started sometime in the 1940s with a fight in the town square and was banned in several of the years that followed. Now sponsored by the town itself, the festival's main event is a messy, tomato-hurling food fight.

Suspect 2—Mary Onette

- Jubilee, Indiana, is between Raymar and Hamerville, Indiana.

- *The Greatest Show on Earth* won the Academy Award for Best Motion Picture in 1952.

- The group Bread & Puppet produced Bread & Puppet's Domestic Resurrection Circus 27 times, 23 of them in the town of Glover, Vermont. The group had three rules about behavior at the Circus—no drugs, no alcohol, no dogs—but they could not control people's behavior outside Bread & Puppet property. Following the death of Michael Sarazin in a fist fight, Bread & Puppet's director, Peter Schumann, announced that there would be no further annual Bread &

Puppet Domestic Resurrection Circus events. An estimated 60,000 people may have attended the last Bread & Puppet Domestic Resurrection Circus in 1998.

Suspect 3—E. (Ellen) Quel-Wright

- Celebration, Florida, is west of Kissimmee, Florida.

- Samuel Goldfish, better known as Samuel Goldwyn, died in 1974.

- The Wife Carrying World Championship is held every July in Sonkajarvi, Finland. The North American Wife Carrying Championship is held in July at the Sunday River Ski Resort in Newry, Maine. First Prize in both contests is the wife's weight in beer.

- The Finnish contest is based on a nineteenth-century practice in which recruits to a band of robbers were forced to run an obstacle course with a sack on their backs as training for stealing women from nearby villages.

Suspect 4—George Gathering Crowd

- Jubilee, Pennsylvania, is east of Tooley Corners, Pennsylvania.

- The International Olympic Committee restored Jim Thorpe's Olympic Medals in 1982. Thorpe died in 1953.

- The Gathering of Nations Powwow is held every April in Albuquerque, New Mexico. Members of more than 500 tribes from all over the United States and Canada gather to dance, sell their crafts and crown Miss Indian World.

The Mystery of the Sabotaged Speaker

The Crime

It was Scrofulous Scum's big chance. Radio station WROT was sponsoring the Hot New Band Competition. The first-place prize was an all-expenses-paid, two-month, 50-city tour of school auditoriums. The band was eager and ready, and as soon as the Scum's lead singer, Rod Wrath, laid into his guitar for the opening riff of "Got No Clue," there was a sudden burst of flame that sent the crowd into an ecstatic round of applause. Unfortunately, that part of the act was not rehearsed. One of the band's badly overloaded and improperly wired speakers had malfunctioned. Without adequate amplification, Scrofulous Scum sounded like any five teenagers playing the same two chords over and over again. They lost the competition.

The Question

Who ruined Scrofulous Scum's big chance at stardom?

The Suspects

Suspect 1—Mabel Rathbone

Mabel Rathbone, Rod Wrath's grandmother, claims to have been born in Moosic, Pennsylvania, which is south of Old Forge, the year that heavy-metal musician John Michael Osbourne was born.

"I knew Rodney and his band could win the competition," Mabel told us with familial pride. "I was proud of him. But I can't deny that I was worried about what would happen if they won. I was only 11 years old when my idol, Charles Hardin Holley, died. He was touring, too. Twenty-two years old, fabulously talented, and his life ended in a midwestern cornfield. It was just like Don McLean said in his song 'American Pie.'" Mabel stopped to wipe a tear from her cheek. "February 3, 1959, was 'the day the music died.'"

"Rodney is the only family I have now that my daughter is gone," she told us. "I've supported him for the past five years with the electrical appliances repair business I took over after my husband left me."

Mabel Rathbone's Alibi: "After I helped the band set up their equipment, I sat down in the audience. In the back of the auditorium," she added. "The decibel level up front is more than my old ears can take. I can tell you this with absolute assurance. That equipment was in proper working order the last time I saw it."

Suspect 2—Melody Maibee

Melody Maibee, a student in the high school's electrical shop and volunteer stagehand for the competition, claims to have been born in Band Mill, Tennessee, which is south of Stinger, the year that *The Broadway Melody* won the Academy Award for Best Motion Picture.

"The minute I saw the sparks, I rushed over to help, but I got there too late," Melody told us. "That speaker was fried. I thought I could fix it in time for the band to stay in the competition, but I was wrong. I'm kind of sorry about that. I was sort of hoping they'd, like, you know, notice me, and be grateful and stuff like that, and then, maybe, I'd sing and they'd realize how well I'd fit in with the band. But those wires were, like, crispy-crittered, if you know what I mean."

"I'm a really good singer," Melody informed us. "I'm sort of a cross between Britney Spears and Selena Quintanilla Perez. My mom wants me to sing with Selena and her band, The Bellezas, someday because she's known as, like, 'The Queen of Baladas,' but I think I'm more like Britney, 'cause, well, first, we both have the same middle name—Jill."

Melody Maibee's Alibi: "I was backstage helping the bands with their stuff."

Suspect 3—Brian Brainard

Brian Brainard, lead singer for Brain Boys, another band in the competition, claims to have been born in Drum, Missouri, which is southeast of Lutesville, the year that *Joyful Noise: Poems for Two Voices* won the Newbery Award.

"Scrofulous Scum is acting like they would have won if their speaker hadn't flamed," Brian Brainard complained. "But the truth is, they weren't that good. Yeah, they were loud. Period. That's all they were."

"Brain Boys is a more cerebral band, which makes us less popular with hoi polloi but puts us in the catbird seat with the judges, most of whom are teachers at the high school. We're like They Might Be Giants, a rock band that most of the time consists of just two guys, John Linnell and John Flansburgh, backed up by tapes and synthesizers. We may not be as hip as the rapper Marshall Bruce Mathers III—you probably know him as Eminem—but, trust me, we're a whole lot better than Scrofulous Scum."

Brian Brainard's Alibi: "I was backstage with my partner, Brian Butler, waiting for our turn to go on. Yeah, we had access to Scrofulous Scum's equipment when they all went out behind the high school for a cigarette before their set," Brian Brainard admitted. "And, yeah, I would have known how to rig it to blow up. My partner and I are really, really smart. But we didn't do it. You know why? We have integrity."

Suspect 4—Eartha Drumm

Eartha Drumm, audiologist for the local school district, claims to have been born in Music, Kentucky, which is northeast of Beetle, the year that Janis Joplin died.

"Do you have any idea what music like Scrofulous Scum's does to young people's hearing?" Eartha asked us. "Former President Bill Clinton now wears hearing aids, in part because he played the saxophone in bands when he was younger. And Peter Townshend, guitarist for The Who, now has to say 'What?' because he didn't have the good sense to wear musician's earplugs every time he played."

"But young people don't want to hear about noise-induced hearing loss," Eartha complained. "They don't believe that listening to loud music damages the tiny hairs in their cochleas and that later in life they won't be able to hear the higher frequencies of sound. It's a constant battle to protect these kids, and I'm getting tired of the effort."

Eartha Drumm's Alibi: "I was backstage measuring the dBA level—that's the 'decibels adjusted' level—of the bands. Scrofulous Scum's dBA was 130. Thank God their amplifier blew up before they inflicted that level of noise on the audience."

The Solution

Melody Maibee wired the speaker incorrectly so she could rush to the rescue, but, in her own words, "I got there too late … I thought I could fix it in time for the band to stay in the competition." Melody thought that her ability to fix the speaker would attract the attention and gratitude of Scrofulous Scum's band members, which would lead to a chance to sing with them, which would lead to stardom. But, again in her own words, "I was wrong."

Information About the Suspects

Suspect 1—Mabel Rathbone

- Moosic, Pennsylvania, is south of Old Forge, Pennsylvania.

- John Michael Osbourne, also known as Ozzy Osbourne, was born in 1948.

- Charles Hardin Holley, lead singer of Buddy Holly and the Crickets (he dropped the E from his name when he started to record music), died in a plane crash on February 3, 1959. He was 22 years old.

- Don McLean's song "American Pie" was about the day Buddy Holly, Ritchie Valens and the Big Bopper died.

Suspect 2—Melody Maibee

- Band Mill, Tennessee, is northeast, not south, of Stinger, Tennessee.

- *The Broadway Melody* won the Academy Award for Best Motion Picture in 1929.

- Selena Quintanilla Perez was known as "The Queen of Tejano." Her band was Selena Y Los Dinos. Melody can't sing with Selena because Selena died in 1995.

- Britney Spears's middle name is Jean, not Jill.

Suspect 3—Brian Brainard

- Drum, Missouri, is southeast of Lutesville, Missouri.

- *Joyful Noise: Poems for Two Voices* won the Newbery Award in 1989.

- They Might Be Giants is a rock band that most of the time consists of two members, John Linnell and John Flansburgh, backed up by tapes and synthesizers.

- Eminem, the rapper, was born Marshall Bruce Mathers III.

Suspect 4—Eartha Drumm

- Music, Kentucky, is northeast of Beetle, Kentucky.

- Janis Joplin died in 1970.

- Former President William Clinton wears hearing aids for a hearing loss that may have been at least partially caused by playing saxophone with bands in his teens without using adequate earplugs.

- Peter Townshend, guitartist for the rock band The Who, has suffered noise-induced hearing loss.

- Frequent exposure to loud music damages the tiny hairs in the ears' cochleas, which eventually leads to an inability to hear the higher frequencies of sound.

- dBA means "decibels adjusted." It is a measurement of noise level.

- Amplified rock music very often registers 110–130 dBA.

The Mystery of the Fraudulent Forward

The Crime

Vector Twain was thrilled to see the size of the crowd that had gathered for the grand opening of Tech-Tok, his new state-of-the-art computer store, but he was baffled by the computer printout the first customers held in their hands. Then, realizing that every person in the crowd of thousands held the same computer printout, Vector Twain panicked and tried to close the store. "They tore the place apart," Vector Twain lamented. "I was between the proverbial rock and a hard place. I couldn't afford to honor the coupons they brought in, but they trashed my store when I refused to. I would have been ruined either way."

The computer message had circulated via e-mail. It read:

I got this coupon because I'm on a mailing list for a new computer store that's about to open, but I want to share it with everyone who loves computers as much as I do. Forward this message to everyone in your address book. Then print out the coupon and go to Tech-Tok's grand opening. I'll see you there!

Directly below the message was an official-looking coupon entitling the bearer to $100 worth of free merchandise on the day of Tech-Tok's grand opening.

The Question

Who spread the e-rumor about free merchandise at Tech-Tok?

The Suspects

Suspect 1—Daemon Dolby

Daemon Dolby, former employee of Tech-Tok, claims to have been born in Apple, Ohio, which is north of Blackjack, the year that Grace Murray Hopper was born.

"Vector got what he deserved this time." Daemon Dolby chuckled. "The miserable double-dealing rat told me he was going to make me manager of the new store, and then, after I put in a huge amount of overtime getting ready for the grand opening, he fired me. He said I wasn't stable enough to work with the public. I wanted to kill him. And, sure, I was capable of pulling off something like this coupon caper, but I didn't. It's not my style. I would have done something more complicated, like attaching the Bear Virus to all his outgoing customer e-mails. You've never heard of the Bear Virus?" Daemon Dolby seemed surprised. "Jeesh! You ought to keep yourself better informed. You ought to check out the virus info on Snopes.com. Here, I'll write it down for you. Bear Virus, also known as JDBGMGR.EXE. If your computer has the Bear file, you've got to get rid of it pronto before it eats your C drive."

Daemon Dolby's Alibi: "I've been spending most of my time at Baud Boolean's store, Talk-Tech, running the Turing Test on his computer equipment. Don't tell me you've never heard of the Turing Test, either? You should take a basic computer course, okay? It's criminal for you to touch a computer knowing as little as you do about the technology. The Turing Test was developed by Alan Turing way back in 1998 to determine whether Internet sites have been placing cookies on your C drive. Baud's letting me do tech maintenance work right now, but he says he'll move me up into a managerial position when one comes open."

Suspect 2—Cookie Cache

Cookie Cache, former wife of Vector Twain, claims to have been born in Dell, Arkansas, which is south of Little Green Store, the year that Tim Berners-Lee was born.

"Everyone falls for an e-rumor sooner or later," Cookie Cache conjectured. "I certainly have, and I'm almost too embarrassed to tell you what it was. I received a forwarded e-mail from a friend claiming that a mixture of Enfalac baby formula and dog food had caused a baby's stomach to explode. I was so alarmed I drove to my sister's house to make sure she wasn't allowing my niece to get near the dog food. She looked it up on Snopes.com, which is what I should have done before I forwarded the message to everyone I knew, and found out it was a hoax. She and my brother-in-law still tease me about that."

"But you want to know whether I had motive and means to perpetrate that nasty little fraud on my ex-husband, don't you?" Cookie Cache asked with refreshing honesty. "Could I have done it? Yes. It wasn't a very sophisticated prank, and I know a fair amount about computers. I'm actually more adept at using and repairing them than Vector is. Did I have a reason to dislike and resent Vector? Yes. This being a community property state, he was awarded half of my assets in the divorce, but he rushed the divorce settlement through so he wouldn't have to share half the profits from his store with me. It was a very Vector move. Did I perpetrate the coupon prank? No. I am a better person than that."

Cookie Cache's Alibi: "I have spent all of my spare time recently rereading Isaac Asimov's science fiction novels. I love his Three Laws of Robotics: 1) A robot may not injure a human being or, by inaction, allow a human being to come to harm; 2) A robot must obey orders given to him by humans except where those orders would conflict with Law 1; and 3) A robot must protect its own existence as long as such protection does not conflict with Laws 1 or 2."

Suspect 3—Baud Boolean

Baud Boolean, owner of rival computer store Talk-Tech, claims to have been born in Gateway, Oregon, which is west of Mecca, the year that Charles Babbage died.

"Whoever pulled the coupon scam knew human nature. Target people's financial self-interest," Baud Boolean advised. "It works every time. Consider the Bill Gates e-mail tracing project. Back in 2001 Gates sent out 500 e-mails promising everything from Applebee's gift certificates to cash payments if the e-mail recipients forwarded the message to other people. A huge number of people did. I'll bet you've received one of those forwards yourself. They're still bouncing around from e-mail inbox to e-mail inbox even though the total payments were capped at $5,000 cash and $5,000 worth of gift certificates. People don't read the fine print at the bottom of the messages. The Urban Legends Reference Pages Web site is always warning people

about being careful on the Internet. Anyway, Gates is still collecting e-mail tracing information, all for a very paltry payout, and the people who are forwarding the messages for him don't get anything at all."

"Of course that makes people angry." Baud Boolean shrugged. "They can't get to Bill Gates, but they could get to Vector Twain. I think that's why the crowd went so nuts when he said he wouldn't honor the coupons. They were angry for all the things they've been promised and never received. And, let's face it, Vector deserved what he got. He's the master of broken promises. Like promising me that his new store wouldn't be in the same mall as mine, wouldn't sell the same line of merchandise, wouldn't undercut my prices."

Baud Boolean's Alibi: "I've spent most of my time lately organizing a book-signing event at Talk-Tech for Dr. Douglas Engelbart. He was a successful orthopedic surgeon who got involved with the computer research lab at the Massachusetts Institute of Technology because he wanted to find a way for people with hand injuries to work with computers, and he ended up inventing the mouse."

Suspect 4—Texel Tweedler

Texel Tweedler, notorious hacker, claims to have been born in Pavillion, Michigan, which is southeast of Suicide Corners, the year that Marc Andreessen was born.

"Yeah, yeah, I know what you want." Texel Tweedler let us into his cluttered apartment. "I did a little jail time for hacking into Pentagon records, so now

I'm suspect number one whenever anything happens on-line. I'll save you a lot of time: I didn't do it. This prank was far too simple for me. You know what I wish I had done?" His eyes sparkled with mischief. "I wish I had been the prankster who spread the rumor that Michael Jackson's phone number can be found in the Universal Product Code on his *Thriller* album. It didn't take long for that rumor to be debunked on the Urban Legends Reference Pages, though. That Barbara Mikkelson is a smart cookie, no computer pun intended."

Texel Tweedler's Alibi: "What have I been doing with my time lately? Well, I've been following in the footsteps of my idol, Steve Wozniak. After founding the Apple Computer Company, then organizing a couple of rock concerts, he became a grade school teacher. That's where it's at, man—holding your hand out to the generation behind you. See what's on the wall over there?" Texel Tweedler pointed to a paper plate on which a childish hand had crayoned "U B D Best Mr. Tweedler." "I was so touched when my class gave me that, I cried."

The Solution

As Baud Boolean pointed out, people get angry when they don't receive what they think they have been promised. Daemon Dolby was angry that he was fired rather than promoted to manager of Vector Twain's new store. Baud Boolean was angry that Vector Twain broke every promise he made not to compete with Boolean's store. Together they concocted the simple, yet devastatingly effective, coupon fraud. They probably started with Talk-Tech's customer e-mail list, but after the first tap of the Send button, the message would have taken on a life of its own. It is probably still circulating on the Web, promising $100 worth of free merchandise to anyone who shows up at the grand opening of a store named Tech-Tok.

Information About the Suspects

Suspect 1—Daemon Dolby

- Apple, Ohio, is southwest, not north, of Blackjack, Ohio.

- Grace Murray Hopper was born in 1906.

- The Bear Virus, also known as the JDBGMGR.EXE virus, is a hoax that cons people into deleting a file that should be on their C drives by convincing them that it is a virus spread by infected e-mail.

- The Turing Test was developed by Alan Turing, but it has nothing to do with cookies on the C drive. It is a method for testing a computer's capacity for sentience, or intelligent thought.

Suspect 2—Cookie Cache

- Dell, Arkansas, is south of Little Green Store, Arkansas.

- Tim Berners-Lee was born in 1955.

- The forwarded e-mail claiming that a mixture of Enfalac baby formula and dog food caused a baby's stomach to explode is a hoax.

- Snopes.com is the on-line address of Urban Legends Reference Pages.

- Isaac Asimov, author of science fiction novels, invented the Three Laws of Robotics. They are: 1) A robot may not injure a human being or, by inaction, allow a human being to come to harm; 2) A robot must obey orders given to him by humans except where those orders would conflict with Law 1; and 3) A robot must protect its own existence as long as such protection does not conflict with Laws 1 or 2.

Suspect 3—Baud Boolean

- Gateway, Oregon, is east, not west, of Mecca, Oregon.

- Charles Babbage died in 1871.

- The Bill Gates e-mail tracing project is a hoax. He never offered cash or Applebee's gift certificates to people who forwarded his message to their friends.

- Dr. Douglas Engelbart led the team that invented the mouse, but he was an electrical engineer, not an orthopedic surgeon, and he worked at the Stanford Research Institute and the Augmentation Research Center in California, not MIT.

Suspect 4—Texel Tweedler

- Pavillion, Michigan, is southeast of Suicide Corners, Michigan.

- Marc Andreessen was born in 1971.

- The rumor that Michael Jackson's phone number can be found in the Universal Product Code on his *Thriller* album is just that—a rumor. The rumor has been debunked on Snopes.com, also known as Urban Legends Reference Pages, which is written by Barbara Mikkelson.

Difficult Mysteries

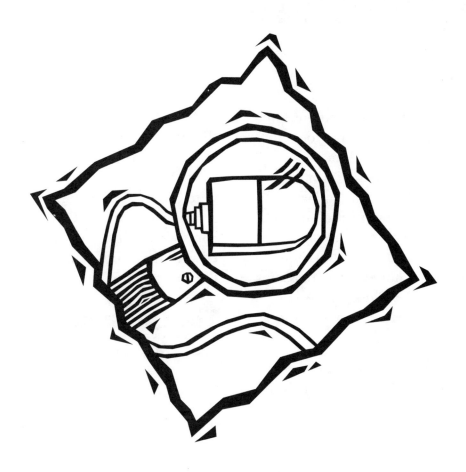

The Mystery of the Filched Fairy Fortune

The Crime

When the caretaker of the Fabulous Folk and Fairy Museum opened the doors in the morning, he discovered the leprechaun's pot o' gold missing from the museum's display. "The museum was being used for the annual Fabulous Folk and Fairy Convention," the caretaker told us. "They were all in the museum sipping mead from honeysuckle blossoms when I left last night. They promised to clean up when they were through, and I guess somebody did."

Fortunately, the coins were returned to the museum by Mrs. McCarey, an elderly widow who lives a block away. "I found the pot o' gold in my garden," Mrs. McCarey told us. "And it was lovely. My sprinkler was spraying a fine mist of water, so there was a brilliant rainbow arcing over the pot. Of course I knew the coins weren't real. They were all imprinted with the words 'United Kingdom of the Imagination.'"

The Question

Who took the leprechaun's pot o' gold?

The Suspects

Suspect 1—Monaciello

Monaciello, whose real name is Mario Pazzesco, claims to have been born in Impruneta, Italy, which is "oh, roughly between Firenze and San Pancrazio," the year that *One Flew Over the Cuckoo's Nest* won the Academy Award for Best Motion Picture.

"You'll have to excuse me, I'm a little drunk." Monaciello pulled his red, hooded garment more closely around himself. "But at least I'm a happy drunk, unlike my countryman Monachicchio, who gets mean when he imbibes."

"I did not take the leprechaun's pot o' gold. Why would I need it?" He waved his hand dismissively. "I have my own gold. Now, if you want to ask about the clothes that have been stolen off clotheslines in these parts ... But you're not asking about that crime, are you, so never mind."

Monaciello's Alibi: "After the mead drinking I went looking for a wine cellar to guard. Finding none, I patronized a local tavern until someone tried to steal my hood. I became alarmed that he might be after my treasure as well and went back to my motel room to sleep off *vostro vino Americano inferiore.*"

Suspect 2—Flitella the Fairy

Flitella the Fairy, whose real name is Frances Vanderhaven, claims to have been born in Moonachie, New Jersey, which is "ringed by those fabulously enchanting cities of Passaic, Hackensack, Newark and Hoboken," the year that *The Funny Little Woman*, illustrated by Blair Lent, won the Caldecott Medal.

"I'm not the real Frances Vanderhaven," Flitella insisted. "I'm a changeling. When the fairies think a human baby is being pampered and fussed over too much, they take the baby to live with them and they leave a fairy baby in its place. Well, I'm the fairy baby that got stuck growing up with humans in New Jersey while the real Frances sipped nectar and bathed with morning dew. I've always been a little bitter about that."

"But I've never stopped looking for my real fairy parents," Flitella continued. "Fairies come in a lot of different guises, from wizened old men to beautiful creatures with butterfly wings. Some of them even look human, like that lovely fairy who returned the pot o' gold today. I saw her when I went for a walk yesterday and thought she might be my true fairy mother, but I didn't disturb her because she was concentrating so hard on coaxing the flowers to grow."

Flitella the Fairy's Alibi: "When the convention's mead-sipping ceremony was over I went for a walk on the beach with Basadone. Have you met him?" Flitella blushed a rich rose pink. "He's the woman-kisser fairy. He rides the noonday breezes and steals kisses, but he's really a gentleman," she insisted. "He found a mermaid's purse on the sand and gave it to me, as he said in Italian, *in cambio di un bacio.* I know you humans think mermaids' purses are egg cases for rays and sharks, but we fairies see the truth."

Suspect 3—Bogeyman

Bogeyman, whose real name is Robert Bogart, claims to have been born in

Boger City, North Carolina, which is "I don't know ... you have to go north and east to get to Pumpkin Center and to Mount Mourne, but Boger City is a lot closer to Pumpkin Center, because I can walk there and I can't walk to Mount Mourne because it's too far and there's water before you get there." He claims to have been born the same year that Joanne Kathleen Rowling was born in Chipping Sodbury.

"I like shiny things," Bogeyman told us. "I like to collect shiny things. Ax blades. I could show you my ax blade collection." He stuck his pudgy finger up his nose. "I like children, too. Children can see me, but grown-ups can't. So I get up close to them in the night and say 'boo,' and they go screaming to their parents, who don't believe I'm there. Heh-heh-heh. I have lots of fun playing with the children."

"I used to have a friend named Andre the Giant. Big, he was. Almost seven feet tall, maybe more. Almost 400 pounds, maybe more. He lived in North Carolina, just like me. But he went away to Paris and never came back," Bogeyman said sadly. "When he left he said, '*Au revoir, mon ami. Essayez d'être gentil.*' If I had enough money I'd go to Paris and look for my friend Andre."

Bogeyman's Alibi: "I was out in the woods looking for will-o'-the-wisps so I could rip the little fairies' wings off. Heh-heh-heh."

Suspect 4—Gerta Weisse

Gerta Weisse, who claims to be a Weisse Frau, also claims to have been born in Loccum, Germany, which is south of Dudinghausen, 200 years after Charles Perrault died.

"There was trouble in the air that night," Gerta told us. "My sister Gretchen and I heard the wailing of a Bean Sidhe, a Native American spirit that foretells death. I was very upset about it. I thought the death might be a child's. I remember telling Gretchen that we had to do something about it. Soup! We could make soup, I told her. Or help the child's family buy medicine."

"My sister cannot ignore children in need," Gerta's sister Gretchen interjected. "She doesn't always know what to do, but she always does something. She called out, '*Schnell! Finden sie einen topf!*' and ran into the woods to find a fairy ring so we could pick mushrooms. But before we could pick enough to make a nourishing soup, we heard that awful Bogeyman crashing around in the underbrush and we fled."

Gerta Weisse's Alibi: "We were traveling around the neighborhood, looking in windows to see if we could find the sick child. Several people seemed upset, but no one seemed close to death. I haven't heard that a child died last night, so perhaps we frightened Death away. I certainly hope so."

The Mystery of the Filched Fairy Fortune

The Solution

Weisse Fraus are very protective of children. Hearing what she thought was the sound of a Banshee wailing in the night, Gerta became frantic at the thought that a child might be near death. Her sister Gretchen said that Gerta could not ignore a child in need. Even though she didn't always know **what** to do, she always did something. Gerta called out for her sister to find a pot in which to collect and cook mushrooms for a nourishing soup, and Gerta grabbed the first pot she saw—the one containing the leprechaun's gold. Failing to find enough mushrooms with which to make a soup, Gerta set out to find a sick child in the neighborhood. Perhaps Gerta left the pot o' gold in Mrs. McCarey's garden because the widow appeared to need financial help. Perhaps Gretchen got tired of lugging it around as she followed her frantic sister from house to house. Both of the Weisse sisters were too distracted to remember details clearly.

Information About the Suspects

Suspect 1—Monaciello

- Impruneta, Italy, is roughly between Firenze and San Pancrazio.

- *One Flew Over the Cuckoo's Nest* won the Academy Award for Best Motion Picture in 1975.

- Monaciello, an Italian fairy, wears a red cloak with a hood. He is almost always drunk, but he is a happy drunk, unlike his countryman Monachicchio, who gets mean when he imbibes.

- Monaciello protects wine cellars, has a treasure and likes to steal clothes.

- *Vostro vino Americano inferiore* means "your inferior American wine."

Suspect 2—Flitella the Fairy

- Moonachie, New Jersey, is surrounded by the following New Jersey cities: Hackensack, Hoboken, Passaic and Newark.

- *The Funny Little Woman,* illustrated by Blair Lent, won the Caldecott Medal in 1973.

- A changeling is a fairy baby who is left in exchange for a human baby that the fairies take to live with them.

- Basadone is an Italian fairy known as the woman-kisser because he rides the noonday breezes and steals kisses.

- A mermaid's purse is an egg case for a ray or shark.

- *In cambio di un bacio* means "in exchange for a kiss."

Suspect 3—Bogeyman

- Boger City, North Carolina, is southwest of both Pumpkin Center and Mount Mourne. There is water to the west of Mount Mourne.

- Joanne Kathleen Rowling was born in 1965 in Chipping Sodbury, England.

- The Bogeyman allegedly can be seen by children but not by adults.

- Andre the Giant was approximately seven feet tall and may have weighed more than 400 pounds. He spent the last part of his life in North Carolina, but he died in Paris.

- *Au revoir, mon ami. Essayez d'être gentil* means "Goodbye, my friend. Try to be nice."

Suspect 4—Gerta Weisse

- A Weisse Frau, literally "white woman," is a German water spirit who protects children.

- Loccum, Germany, is northwest, not south, of Dudinghausen, Germany.

- Charles Perrault died in 1703. Gerta Weisse was born 200 years later, in 1903.

- A Bean Sidhe is an Irish banshee who foretells death, not a Native American spirit.

- *Schnell! Finden sie einen topf!* means "Quick! Find a pot!"

The Mystery of the Pilfered Pyrotechnics

The Crime

The people of Paraíso en la Tierra know how to celebrate Día de los Muertos. They decorate family graves, tell stories about deceased loved ones, and leave offerings for their spirits. They also eat sugary skulls and skeletons, share *pan de muerto* at family dinners and end the final day of the festivities with a grand *castillo*.

This year's *castillo* was rumored to be the biggest, brightest, most complicated *castillo* ever built in Paraíso en la Tierra. Unfortunately, it never had a chance to illuminate the night sky. It was last seen in its storage shed at noon the day before the culminating day of the Día de los Muertos festivities. The neighboring town of Cielo en la Tierra had a spectacular *castillo* that, when described to the builders of Paraíso en la Tierra's *castillo*, seemed suspiciously identical to their own creation, but the political leaders of Cielo en la Tierra refused to divulge the origins of their display.

The Question

What happened to Paraíso en la Tierra's *castillo*?

The Suspects

Suspect 1—Solymar Salud

Solymar Salud, physician, claims to have been born in Doctor Arroyo, in the state of Nuevo León, which is north of the Mexican state of San Luis Potosi, the year that *Sticks and Bones* written by David Rabe, won the Tony Award for Best Play.

"Oh, dear, yes, *el castillo*." Doctor Salud sighed. "The Castle. It is the climax of fiesta celebrations in small Mexican towns like this, and it is incredibly exciting. It is a 20- to 30-foot-tall maze of *carrizo* to which are attached Roman candles and Catherine wheels and rockets, everything connected to a tangle of fuses, which the *cohetero* lights with his cigarette. You Americans are used to a level of safety in your public fireworks displays that does not exist in a town like this. Our pyrotechnics are often crude and unpredictable and dangerously close to spectators."

Solymar Salud's Alibi: "I spent the afternoon at the cemetery creating an *ofrenda* at my parents' graves. I left marigolds, candles, my mother's favorite incense and a bowl of my father's favorite food, *arroz con pollo*. Then I went back to my office to unpack the extra bandages and sutures and antiseptics I had ordered. I expected a rush of burns and wounds from too much *calaverada* the following evening, but that didn't happen. I was enormously relieved when the *castillo* was discovered missing," Dr. Salud admitted candidly. "Día de los Muertos has enough dead to honor without creating more."

Suspect 2—Victor Viaje

Victor Viaje, travel agent, was born on the Riviera Maya, in the state of Quintana Roo, where, he says, "*El castillo* also means the pyramid at Chichén Itzá." He claims to have been born "on the very day that 47-year-old Frida Kahlo died, officially of a pulmonary thrombosis."

"What do you Americans know about *Estados Unidos Mexicanos*?" Victor Viaje demanded bluntly. "Nothing! Less than nothing, because what you think you know is wrong. You think we're all wearing sombreros and strumming guitars, then you are stunned to find 20 million people in Mexico City. When people ask me to arrange accommodations for them in old Mexico, I'm tempted to send them to the Mexico that existed before the Treaty of Guadalupe Hidalgo—somewhere in Utah. Wouldn't that be a surprise?" he asked with cynical amusement. "But I'm a businessman, and I know what people want. They want me to send them to what they think of as old Mexico, so I send them to Paraíso en la Tierra, where they are safe most of the year, except for Día de los Muertos, when they drink too much and get too close to the *castillo*. It's only a matter of time before one of the foolish *turistas* is injured."

Victor Viaje's Alibi: "I was in Paraíso en la Tierra for Día de los Muertos, but I tried to maintain what you Americans call a low profile. One of my clients was there—a particularly obnoxious personal injury lawyer—and I didn't want him to see me. He complains about everything, and I didn't want to hear about his dissatisfactions while I was on vacation myself. If you want to know how I felt about the theft of the *castillo*, I was relieved," Victor Viaje admitted. "With my luck, that fool lawyer would have gotten his hand blown off and come looking to sue me for his own stupidity."

Suspect 3—Señora Cara de la Pasa

Señora Cara de la Pasa, longtime resident of Paraíso en la Tierra, was born in

El Rosario de Abajo, which she claims is located in the same state as Tepeyac—the hill where the Virgin of Guadalupe first appeared. She claims to have been born 50 years before Alfonso García Robles shared the Nobel Peace Prize with Adolfo Pérez Esquivel.

"I disapprove of it all," the elderly Señora Cara de la Pasa said bluntly. "The old ways are heathen ways. Día de los Muertos is an ancient Mexican holiday devoted to the Aztec gods Mictecacihuatl, the Lord of Rebirth, and Huitzilopochtli, the God of Harvest. Eating candy skulls and skeletons is a symbolic way of perpetuating the ancient practice of human sacrifice to please the gods of agriculture. All the dancing in the street, the drinking, the carousing, the *castillo* ... Where is our Lord's place in all of this? Or the Virgin of Guadalupe? In their celebration of the pagan Día de los Muertos, the people of Paraíso en la Tierra have reduced the following day, the feast day of the Virgin of Guadalupe, to a day to recover from their hangovers."

Señora Cara de la Pasa's Alibi: "I spent the day asking God, as I ask him every day, to make me an instrument of his good works on Earth. I fasted and prayed until noon, when I went outside to scold a group of inebriated young men who were stealing figs from my tree. I threw a rock at them and threatened to call the police if they continued to torment me. When they merely laughed I gave them money to go away in order to gain the peace I needed to return to my prayers."

Suspect 4—Pancho Barracho

Pancho Barracho, leader of a band of local youths, claims to have been born in General Bravo, Mexico, which is south of Fandanguillo, "which, I am sure you know, is the birthplace of the famous Mexican dancer Elysia Diomedia," the year that Octavio Paz won the Nobel Peace Prize.

"I saw Cielo en la Tierra's *castillo*," Pancho Barracho admitted. "It was *maravilloso*. Better than any *castillo* Paraíso en la Tierra has ever done, or could do. No wonder the people of Cielo en la Tierra don't want to reveal who made it. They don't want Paraíso en la Tierra stealing his services away. The people of this town are like that. I'll tell you why I was in Cielo en la Tierra. My friends and I were called *hombres sin valor* once too often by the so-called *bueno* people of this town. We drink atole, okay? What is the harm in that? It was given to us by the goddess Mayahuel, so to drink it is to honor the old ways and the old gods of our people. And it gives a man strength so he can have many sons. Not like pulque." Pancho Barracho made a face. "Corn and milk and sugar and cinnamon and chocolate—pulque is a baby's drink. A drink for people like Señora Cara de la Pasa. But I won't ridicule the señora, not today. She gave me and my *amigos* the money to buy our atole. She didn't say it was for atole, exactly," Pancho Barracho admitted. "She said it was the means for us to better the lives of those who live in this town. Her meaning was clear enough. She wanted us to take our celebrating somewhere else. So we did."

Pancho Barracho's Alibi: "My friends and I left for Cielo en la Tierra the night before and didn't return until the night after the *castillo* celebration. We stayed with my friend Luis Fernando's cousin, who is the mayor of Cielo en la Tierra. There are some who appreciate a group of fine, strong men with the will to celebrate the goodness of life. There is a bigger world than Paraíso en la Tierra."

The Solution

Pancho Barracho and his band of fellow revelers had discovered a way to get money to buy pulque. They harassed Señora Cara de la Pasa until she gave them money to go away. Perhaps they suggested that for a somewhat larger amount they could ensure there would be no *castillo* to disrupt the next night's peace, or perhaps it was Señora Cara de la Pasa's idea. Regardless of whose idea it was, "her meaning was clear enough," according to Pancho Barracho. "She said it was the means for us to better the lives of those who live in this town ... She wanted us to take our celebrating somewhere else. So we did."

Pancho Barracho and his friends left town between the last time the *castillo* was seen (noon, November 1) and the time it was discovered missing (the evening of November 2). They were probably warmly welcomed by Pancho's friend's cousin, the mayor of Cielo en la Tierra. Perhaps they were given even more money with which to purchase even more pulque in gratitude for the *castillo maravilloso* they brought with them.

Information About the Suspects

Suspect 1—Solymar Salud

- Doctor Arroyo is located in the state of Nuevo León, Mexico, which is north of the state of San Luis Potosi, Mexico.

- *Sticks and Bones,* written by David Rabe, won the Tony Award for Best Play in 1972.

- *El castillo* (the castle) is a 20- to 30-foot-tall maze of *carrizo* (reeds) to which are attached Roman candles and Catherine wheels and rockets, everything connected to a tangle of fuses.

- *A cohetero,* which translates as "missile specialist," is the rocket man who lights the *castillo.*

- Mexican fireworks displays are sometimes dangerously close to spectators.

- During Día de los Muertos, people leave *ofrenda* (offerings to the dead), which may include candles and marigolds and objects that were particularly pleasing to the deceased.

- *Arroz con pollo* means "rice with chicken."

- *Calaverada* means "recklessness."

- Día de los Muertos, Day of the Dead, is a holiday that honors deceased relatives, ancestors and friends.

Suspect 2—Victor Viaje

- The Riviera Maya is in the Mexican state of Quintana Roo.

- *El castillo* is a pyramid at Chichén Itzá—Mayan ruins that are also in Quintana Roo.

- Frida Kahlo died in 1954, officially of pulmonary thrombosis.

- *Estados Unidos Mexicanos* is Mexico's official name.

- Mexico City, the world's largest city, has a population of more than 20 million people.

- The Treaty of Guadalupe Hidalgo, signed in 1848, ceded Mexican land in what is now California and Nevada, most of Arizona and New Mexico and parts of Wyoming, Utah and Colorado to the United States in exchange for $15 million.

- *Turistas* means "tourists."

Suspect 3—*Señora Cara de la Pasa*

- El Rosario de Abajo is located in the state of Baja California. Tepeyac, the hill where the Virgin of Guadalupe first appeared, is located in Mexico City.

- Alfonso García Robles shared the 1982 Nobel Peace Prize with Alva Myrdal. (Señora Cara de la Pasa was born 50 years earlier, in 1932.)

- Argentinian Adolfo Pérez Esquival won the Nobel Peace Prize in 1980, not 1982.

- Día de los Muertos is a blend of ancient Mexican beliefs and Christian beliefs.

- The original Aztec holiday was presided over by Mictecacihuatl, but she was a goddess, not a god, and she was known as Lady of the Dead, not the Lord of Rebirth.

- Huitzilopochtli was a major Aztec war god, whose name translates as one of the following: Sinister Hummingbird, Blue Hummingbird or Hummingbird on the Left. He was not the God of Harvest.

- The feast day of the Virgin of Guadalupe is celebrated on December 12.

- Día de los Muertos is celebrated between October 31 and November 2.

Suspect 4—*Pancho Barracho*

- General Bravo, Mexico, is south of Fandanguillo, but the famous Mexican dancer Elysia Diomedia was not born there. *Elysia diomedia,* the Mexican Dancer, is a sea slug.

- Octavio Paz won the Nobel Prize in Literature, not the Nobel Peace Prize, in 1990.

- *Maravilloso* means "marvelous."

- *Hombres sin valor* means "men without value."

- *Bueno* means "good."

- *Amigos* means "friends."

- Atole is a beverage made of ground corn, milk or water, sugar, cinnamon and chocolate.

- Pulque, reportedly discovered by the goddess Mayahuel, is a beverage made by fermenting the sap of certain types of agave plants. It is said to give a man strength so he can have many sons.

The Mystery of the Tainted Tea

The Crime

Mr. and Mrs. Spaulding Teasdale had come to the Inner I Tea Room for an afternoon respite from their busy schedules. Spaulding Teasdale had spent the morning attempting to merge several fast-food businesses into one large conglomerate called MacTacoColonel, and he planned to spend the afternoon playing golf with a state senator and a local judge. Gloriosa Teasdale had spent the morning getting her companion Yiparella's hair trimmed and tinted, and she looked forward to a busy afternoon of buying Yiparella a travel wardrobe. Yiparella looked forward to a plate of tea sandwiches and a nap in the back window of the Teasdales' chauffeured limousine.

Suddenly, tragedy struck. Yiparella barked ferociously at thin air, trembled with agitation, whimpered, then fell dead across a cup of Renew Vital Juices tea.

The Question

Who killed Yiparella?

The Suspects

Suspect 1—Spaulding Teasdale

Spaulding Teasdale, business mogul, claims to have been born in Teaneck, New Jersey, which is east of the city that bears the name of the United States' twentieth president. He was born the year that *Teahouse of the August Moon* won the Pulitzer Prize for Best Drama.

"My wife is unavailable to speak with you," Spaulding Teasdale informed us. "She has been sedated. Grief over the dog," he added with a tight-lipped smile. "It was a shih tzu, a breed that originated in China. I'm sure you've seen one. They're all the rage now. They're effete little rug rodents with absolutely no purpose beyond sitting around and being pampered. They don't hunt or guard or fetch. They **do** shed. They do that extremely well. They have a coat of long hair over a second, woolly, undercoat, which gives them twice as much hair to leave on the furniture. Yiparella was arrogant, obstinate and stubborn, and she wheezed and snored when she slept, which was a considerable amount of the time. My wife said the dog reminded her of me when we first met. She certainly treated it like she treated me when we first met. She even called it the same pet name she used to call me—*mon petit chiot amusant.*"

Spaulding Teasdale's Alibi: "I wasn't having a good day. The merger talks had not gone well. Gloriosa had insisted that we meet in that dreadfully pretentious tea room, and she ordered the tea she thought I should have. I would have preferred a simple lapsang souchon, or, better yet, a good old cuppa Joe. Instead I got something that smelled so vile I didn't think I was going to be able to drink it, but I knew Gloriosa wouldn't be in a pleasant mood if I didn't drink it. Then Tia walked over to my table and ..." Spaulding Teasdale flushed an unexpected crimson. "I don't understand women," he confided. "I never have. They are as inscrutable as the Sphinx of Giza. But, to return to your question, Yiparella started yapping and growling, and she died. Just like that."

"Not exactly just like that," Spaulding Teasdale amended. "I should tell you one more thing. There was a moment when Gloriosa was distracted by the strange behavior of the person who should have been waiting on us. I took that moment to pour my tea into Yiparella's cup. I knew the dog wouldn't be bothered by the smell. She ate and drank anything. That tea was meant for me," Spaulding Teasdale said bluntly. "I was the one who was supposed to die."

Suspect 2—Tia Totaller

Tia Totaller, a chemist, was born in Tea, South Dakota, which, she says, is "in the southeast corner of the state where South Dakota, Nebraska, Iowa and Minnesota all come into close proximity and all look pretty much the same." She claims to have been born 10 years after Albert Francis Blakeslee died.

"I looked up from my Inner Child Revival Tea, and **he** was there. Spaldy," Tia Totaller explained. "We dated for seven years. I thought we were in love. I thought that all I had to do was offer him patient emotional support until he got past his fear of commitment. Then he met **her,** and they were married three weeks later. But it's all right." She smiled tightly. "Why would I be bitter? I have a good job, a nice apartment and three cats. It's a full life."

"I am a senior chemist for Wild Alkaloids, Inc.," Tia Totaller told us. "It's a company that makes nutritional supplements from organic sources. Right now I'm heading up a team studying the possibilities of jimsonweed. The jimsonweed plant contains alkaloids, particularly atropine, hyoscyamine and hyoscine, which is otherwise known as scopolamine, which, when mixed with morphine, produces Twilight Sleep. I'm going to recommend that we don't market any jimsonweed derivatives. Side effects of ingesting the plant include agitation, confusion and the possibility of death. Those are hardly the reactions a vitamin company wants to produce in its customers."

Tia Totaller's Alibi: "It was all very odd. I wanted to show Spaldy that I had gotten over him, so I walked over to his table to say hello. But when I got there I leaned down and kissed him. I don't know what made me do that." Tia Totaller blushed a vivid crimson. "I heard Spaldy's wife suck in a breath of air. I heard that little rodent dog of hers slurping something under the table. There was a tall boy shuffling around, banging chairs out of his way and looking in the corners. The woman behind the counter was saying something I couldn't quite catch, but it sounded obscene. I turned around and walked back to my table as slowly as I could. That took an enormous amount of self-control," Tia Totaller admitted. "I left some money on the table, gathered up my purse and my briefcase and the magazine I'd been reading. I was almost to the door when the dog started barking ferociously. It was incredibly agitated. I would guess it was hallucinating. Then it whimpered and fell to the floor in what appeared to be a seizure. I went over to examine it, but Spaldy's wife shoved me away. She said, 'You've done enough already. Leave my precious darling alone!' So I did."

Suspect 3—Mandrake God I Ching Jones

Mandrake God I Ching Jones, son of the owner of the Inner I Tea Room, claims to have been born in Teaticket, Massachusetts, which is northeast of Wood's Hole on the island of Nantucket, the year that River Phoenix starred in the movie *Running on Empty.*

"Call me Manny, please," Mandrake Jones requested as he flopped down on a chair in the empty tea room. "Mom inhabits a higher astral plain. You know, the same astral plain where Frank Zappa went around naming his sons Moon Unit, Dweezil and Ahmet Rodan. Both of them should be arrested for child abuse. Well, yeah, **I have** been arrested," Mandrake Jones admitted. "A little pot, that's all."

"The way my mom reacted, you'd think I was the biggest drug user this side of Mars. Like **she** isn't a druggie herself," he said derisively. "She's totally addicted to the most commonly used mind-altering drug in the world. Good old $C_{10}H_{14}N_2$. Man, take away her coffee and she's a total mess—jitters, irritability, hypersensitivity to sound and light. Then, hello, latte! As soon as her nervous system feels that caffeine coming, it calms right down. But **she** doesn't have a problem because that stuff's legal. Give me a break!"

Mandrake God I Ching Jones's Alibi: "I was here in the tea room. The two conditions of my probation are that I work for my mother and that I don't use any marijuana. I promised, so I am, but I don't have to be happy about it, do I? Anyway, I'm kind of confused about what happened that afternoon. I had made myself a cup of tea. Then I was looking for something I had lost. Then that dog started barking at the air like it saw a ghost or something. Man, it was creepy." Mandrake Jones shivered with the memory. "Then the dog sort of turned around like it was going to bite its tail, and shook a bit, and then it dropped dead. Bumph! Right there on top of one of the super-size lotus cups my mother imported from Tibet."

Suspect 4—Marta Teebeutel

Marta Teebeutel, employee of the Inner I Tea Room, was born in Unternogg, Germany, which, she says, is "very close to the border of Germany and the Czech Republic, so close I consider myself half-Czech." She also claims to have been born exactly 150 years after William Tuke established the first hospital for the mentally ill in New York City.

"Do you need someone to work for you?" Marta Teebeutel asked. "I am a good worker and I would leave this job in a minute if I had another one. Frau Jones is off here and there buying exotic tea ingredients, leaving me and her son to watch the shop alone. Mandrake is—how you say?—*unbrauchbarer. Zu viel rauch, rauch, rauch, jetzt ist er ein unbrauchbarer junge.*"

"We cannot sell just a few kinds of tea, oh, no," Marta Teebeutel continued her complaint. "We sell at least a hundred kinds, each one specially blended to cure whatever ailment you think you have. To relieve stress, I am supposed to blend one of the plants from the Mint family, like the Common Tansy or Blueberry, with one of the members of the Aster family, like basil or horehound. There is a chart showing the different blends, but it's hard to read. And that afternoon was very busy in the shop. And Mandrake ..." Marta Teebeutel gave a snort of disgust. "Instead of waiting on the customers, he was bumbling around the tea room looking for something he had lost. And that horrible Mrs. Teasdale was demanding service and threatening to get me fired, as if that was a threat. Right at that moment, I would have welcomed being fired. She ordered three very complicated tea blends. Skin Glow Luminous for herself, Renew Vital Juices for her husband and Healthy Hair and Nails for that creature of hers. Frau Jones would have had a fit if she had seen a dog drinking out of one of her tea cups, but Frau Jones wasn't here, was she?"

Marta Teebeutel's Alibi: "I'll tell you the truth, but please don't tell Frau Jones." Marta Teebeutel confessed. "I didn't follow the chart when I made the teas. I was busy and I didn't think the customers would know the difference between one tea blend and another. I used a few of the tins of tea Frau Jones makes up for our customers to take home. One of them had fallen onto the floor, and I picked that one up and used it, too. The tea I made with that one smelled malodorous, but a lot of the teas smell bad, so I didn't think anything was amiss until the dog died. I think Frau Jones has finally killed something with her ridiculous herbal concoctions."

The Solution

No one meant to kill the dog or harm Spaulding Teasdale. Mandrake Jones had promised not to use marijuana, but he hadn't promised not to use other drugs. He was experimenting with jimsonweed, a local plant that could be brewed into a tea. He had had a cup of it the afternoon of Yiparella's death, so he was confused and agitated by the time the Teasdales arrived. But he wasn't so confused that he didn't realize he had misplaced the jimsonweed and the tea tin in which it was contained. He was in a panic looking for it. Unfortunately, Marta Teebeutel found it first and used it to brew Spaulding Teasdale's Renew Vital Juices tea. It's a good thing he poured his tea into the dog's cup, though it probably wouldn't have killed Spaulding Teasdale. The dose was lethal to Yiparella because she was so small.

Information About the Suspects

Suspect 1—Spaulding Teasdale

- James Garfield was the twentieth president of the United States.

- Teaneck, New Jersey, is east of Garfield, New Jersey.

- *Teahouse of the August Moon* won the Pulitzer Prize for Best Drama in 1954.

- The shih tzu breed of dog originated in China. Shih-tzus have a coat of long hair over a second, woolly, undercoat. They can be arrogant, obstinate and stubborn. They can also wheeze and snore when they sleep.

- *Mon petit chiot amusant* means "my amusing little puppy."

- Lapsang souchon is Chinese black tea.

- A cuppa Joe is slang for coffee.

Suspect 2—Tia Totaller

- Tea, South Dakota, is in the southeast corner of the state, where South Dakota, Nebraska, Iowa and Minnesota are in close proximity to one another.

- Albert Francis Blakeslee died in 1954. Tia Totaller was born 10 years later, in 1964.

- The jimsonweed plant contains alkaloids, particularly atropine, hyoscyamine and hyoscine. Hyoscine is also known as scopolamine, which, when mixed with morphine, produces Twilight Sleep, a pain amnesiac once popularly used during childbirth.

- Side effects of ingesting jimsonweed include agitation, confusion and the possibility of death.

Suspect 3—Mandrake God I Ching Jones

- Teaticket, Massachusetts, is northeast of Wood's Hole, Massachusetts, but neither is on the island of Nantucket.

- River Phoenix starred in the movie *Running on Empty* in 1988.

- Frank Zappa did name three of his children Moon Unit, Dweezil and Ahmet Rodan, but only Dweezil and Ahmet Rodan are sons. Moon Unit is his daughter.

- Caffeine is the most commonly used mind-altering drug in the world.

- $C_{10}H_{14}N_2$ is the chemical formula of nicotine. Caffeine's chemical formula is $C_8H_{10}N_4O_2$.

- Symptoms of caffeine withdrawal include headaches, fatigue and depression.

- Caffeine stimulates the central nervous system. It does not calm it.

Suspect 4—Marta Teebeutel

- Unternogg, Germany, is close to the border of Germany and Austria, not the Czech Republic.

- William Tuke, who founded a hospital for the mentally ill in England, not New York City, died in 1822. Marta Teebeutel was born 150 years later, in 1972.

- *Unbrauchbarer. Zu viel rauch, rauch, rauch, jetzt ist er ein unbrauchbarer junge* means "useless. Too much smoke, smoke, smoke, now he is a useless boy."

- The Common Tansy belongs to the Asteraceae family, which is commonly called any of the following: aster family, daisy family or sunflower family.

- The Blueberry belongs to the Ericaceae family, which is commonly called any of the following: heath family, heather family or rhododendron family.

- Basil and horehound are members of the mint family.

Additional Information:

- Jimsonweed is usually ingested in the form of an herbal tea infusion.

- Jimsonweed leaves have an unpleasant odor.

- Symptoms of jimsonweed ingestion include hallucinations, delirium, blurred vision, dilated pupils, trembling, confusion, agitation, combative behavior, seizures, coma and possible death.

- Symptoms can appear within a few minutes or up to a few hours after ingestion.

The Mystery of the Burgled Baubles

The Crime

Sissy St. Claire was hysterical. "They stole our necklaces! I'll have their ugly two-faced heads for this!"

The necklaces in question were strings of cheap, shiny, metallic beads that were to have been tossed off the St. Claire Street Krewe float during the Mardi Gras parade. "I asked my assistant, Larkie, to lay them out on the table in the back courtyard of my home," Sissy explained. "My driver was going to get the float and bring it around to the back entrance so Larkie could put all of the necklaces into a large treasure chest on the float. I was delayed at the hairdresser's shop. When I realized I didn't have enough time to pick up my Queen of Hearts costume, I called Larkie and asked her to dash over to the dressmaker for me, and, even though the errand should have taken half an hour at most, that stupid girl was gone for hours. When I got home, most of the necklaces were gone. Oh, we

recovered some. Whoever perpetrated the actual theft must have been a clumsy ox because beads were dropped on the sidewalk and draped over shrubbery, but we didn't recover enough of them to fill the treasure chest. We're going to look like fools, running out of beads to throw before the parade has barely started."

"I know someone from the Daughters of the Mermaids Krewe did this," Sissy insisted. "I found a doubloon with their symbol on it on my patio. I'm going to make sure that everyone in New Orleans knows what kind of low-lying bayou scum Coralie Chantal lets into her krewe. When I'm through, she won't be welcome at any masquerade ball in this city."

The Question

Who stole the Mardi Gras beads from the St. Claire Street Krewe?

The Suspects

Suspect 1—Coralie Chantal

Coralie Chantal, leader of the Daughters of the Mermaids Krewe, was born in Birdie, Georgia, which, she says, is "about three miles south of Sunny Side if you walk it, but 10 if you drive," the year Tippi Hedren starred in the movie *The Birds*.

"Give me a break!" Coralie Chantal said impatiently. "I did not steal Sissy St. Claire's pathetically tawdry baubles. According to Sissy, they were stolen on Shrove Tuesday, otherwise known as Fat Tuesday, or, as we say in French, Mardi Gras, which is the day before Ash Wednesday, and you know what that means, don't you, *ma petite renoncule?* It means that Lent was about to begin. As soon as Lent began there would be no more parades, no more masked balls, no more dancing in the streets, no more **fun**. Why on earth would I sacrifice a minute of Mardi Gras's delicious bacchanalia in order to go skulking through the bushes stealing plastic jewelry?"

"Sissy is jealous of me," Coralie Chantal insisted. "I am 100 percent more imaginative and creative than she is, and everybody in this city knows that. For instance, her krewe throws mediocre, mass-produced necklaces to the crowds. I make sure my krewe has something special. I design a special Mardi Gras doubloon every year. I based this year's design on the symbols on the reverse side of the Great Seal of the United States. You know what I'm talking about—that pyramid with the big eye at the top of it. The pyramid is supposed to signify strength and duration, and the eye is Providence,

which can be God, if that's what you believe in, or just, well, good luck or something. I left out the words over the eye, *annuit coeptis,* because one of the women in my krewe said that was Latin for 'it has favored our undertakings,' and I thought that sounded like something a funeral home would have on its motto. But the design makes a real pretty doubloon, don't you think?" she asked, dropping several into our hands.

Coralie Chantal's Alibi: "I was having my hair done, just like half the other women in New Orleans."

Suspect 2—Larkie St. Claire

Larkie St. Claire, Sissy St. Claire's assistant, claims to have been born in Kaw City, Oklahoma, which is northwest of Okay, Oklahoma, 20 years after Paul Newman and Geraldine Page starred in the movie *Sweet Bird of Youth*.

"I'm actually Sissy St. Claire's cousin," Larkie murmured nervously as she led us to Sissy's courtyard. "My mother thought it would be a good idea if I came to New Orleans and stayed with Sissy for a while so I could experience a larger, more exciting world and develop some social graces, and maybe meet someone nice. I'm not very good at talking with people. Sissy gets upset with me. She thinks I'm a country bumpkin. And I am. I know I am."

"I hate it here so much!" she admitted with a cry. "I'm so lonely. The only thing I like about New Orleans is the birds. Sissy doesn't like me to feed them, but I do anyway. The birds are the only creatures in this city that like me." Larkie St. Claire pulled a dinner roll from her pocket and several birds with iridescent black plumage and white wing patches landed at her feet. "Pica pica," she identified them easily. "The black-billed magpie. They're relatives of jays and crows. They're very smart birds. They even recognize people. Sometimes they divebomb Sissy, but they never attack me."

Larkie St. Claire's Alibi: "I didn't mean to stay away so long," she said. "I was on my way to the dressmaker's shop when I thought I saw a common nighthawk. I was so startled I let out a cry, and a man standing nearby said, 'Did you see that? That was a goatsucker, wasn't it?' Of course it was! He was absolutely right! The common nighthawk is a member of the order Caprimulgiformes. Even though the common nighthawk is more crepuscular than the other members of the family, which tend to be more nocturnal, seeing it in the middle of the afternoon, in absolutely broad daylight, was very strange. The man, whose name turned out to be Etienne, said its nest probably had been disturbed by some fool making too much noise, but he thought it was an omen. And then he said some other things." Larkie's cheeks were suffused with a bright rose pink. "And we stopped at a nearby cafe and had a chicory coffee and a beignet. And then I remembered Sissy's costume and ran out of the shop before I could give Etienne my address or phone number, but, even then, Sissy got back to the house before I did and she was furious with me for leaving the necklaces unguarded." Larkie St. Claire tossed the last of the shredded roll to the several dozen birds that were pecking at her feet. "Do you think Etienne will be able to find me?" she asked plaintively.

Suspect 3—Madame Adora Visage

Madame Adora Visage, mask maker, claims to have been born in Birdsnest, Virginia, which is about 50 miles southwest of Chincoteague Island, the year that *Finders Keepers* won the Caldecott Medal.

"Come in, come in." Madame Visage invited us into her shop. "I have been expecting you. I see everyone sooner or later. You're looking for masks? Feather masks? Venetian masks? Animal masks? Ah, no ..." She stopped to examine our faces more closely. "You want something a little more interesting, don't you? Come with me." She flicked a soupçon of pink powder into a nearby candle flame. "To appease the spirits," she explained as she pushed a colorful bead curtain aside and led us more deeply into her dark shop.

"Death masks," she explained, gesturing to the unnerving faces that hung from every wall. "I studied at Madame Tussaud's Wax Museum in New York. Perhaps you saw Whoopi Goldberg? I assisted with that wax figure. Well, no, she wasn't dead at the time. It's not like the old days when Madame Tussaud made death masks of King Louis XVI and his queen, Marie Antoinette, from their severed heads. There are so few severed heads anymore. *Malheureusement.*"

Madame Adora Visage's Alibi: "I don't deny that I can always use beads and baubles for my masks. Nor do I deny that I am something of an opportunist about using found materials," she admitted candidly. "But if the theft occurred on Shrove Tuesday, I didn't do it. I was right here in my shop turning out dozens of magpie masks for a last-minute order from the Birds of a Feather Krewe."

Suspect 4—Armand Bonhomie

Armand Bonhomie, Sissy St. Claire's neighbor, claims to have been born in Birdsboro, Pennsylvania, which is about 12 miles southeast of Wyomissing, the year that *To Kill a Mockingbird* won the Pulitzer Prize for Fiction.

"So Sissy has a new little drama in her life, has she?" Armand Bonhomie asked rhetorically. "It's always *sturm und drang* in the St. Claire household. Someone has cheated Sissy. Someone is stalking Sissy. A few weeks ago she accused me of watching her from my window. Trust me, I have no interest in watching Sissy St. Claire. I was actually watching the birds. There are an astounding number in the neighborhood these days. I think that pretty little Larkie feeds them when the old crow's back is turned. Magpies mostly, but there are a few mockingbirds.

There's one little *oiseau de raillerie* that sits outside my window and imitates my singing. It's quite amusing, really."

"Ah, yes, **I do** sing professionally. Are you familiar with Gioachino Rossini's opera *La Gazza Ladra*? It's not one of his most famous works, not like his 1829 opera, *Guillaume Tell,* but it's an interesting piece, perfect for performing in a small opera house with a small orchestra. It's a powerful work, based as it is on a disturbing travesty of justice, though the opera has a much happier ending than the real event."

Armand Bonhomie's Alibi: "I was here singing with Giovanni Gherardini. That is what I have named my little mockingbird friend, in honor of the lovely Milanese doctor and poet who wrote the words for *La Gazza Ladra.*"

The Solution

All of the suspects are telling the truth. None of them stole Sissy St. Claire's beads. But there are other thieves afoot in Sissy St. Claire's neighborhood. To be more precise, there are other thieves a-wing. The magpies that Larkie's daily feedings have attracted in ever-greater numbers are notorious for absconding with shiny objects. Attracted to the shiny beads, the birds made off with as many necklaces as they could before Sissy St. Claire arrived home.

Information About the Suspects

Suspect 1—Coralie Chantal

- Birdie, Georgia, is about three miles south of Sunny Side, Georgia, but, according to Mapquest's driving directions, it is about 10 miles away by car.

- Tippi Hedren starred in the movie *The Birds* in 1963.

- Mardi Gras is French for "Fat Tuesday" or "Fatty Tuesday," also known as Shrove Tuesday. It is the day before Ash Wednesday, which is the beginning of Lent in the Christian faith.

- *Ma petite renoncule* means "my little buttercup."

- The pyramid and eye are symbols on the reverse side of the Great Seal of the United States. The pyramid signifies strength and durability.

- The eye signifies Providence, which many believe to be a symbol for God.

- *Annuit coeptis* is Latin for "it [Providence] has favored our undertakings."

Suspect 2—Larkie St. Claire

- Kaw City, Oklahoma, is northwest of Okay, Oklahoma.

- The movie *Sweet Bird of Youth*, starring Paul Newman and Geraldine Page, was released in 1962. Larkie was born 20 years later, in 1982.

- Pica pica, the black-billed magpie, is a relative of jays and crows. It has iridescent black plumage and white wing patches. Magpies are intelligent birds, and may recognize the people who feed them.

- The common nighthawk is a member of the order Caprimulgiformes, also known as goatsuckers because it was once thought the bird drank goats' milk in the night. Most goatsuckers are nocturnal, but the common nighthawk is crepuscular—it is active at twilight and daybreak.

Suspect 3—Madame Adora Visage

- Birdsnest, Virginia, is about 50 miles southwest of Chincoteague Island, Virginia.

- *Finders Keepers* won the Caldecott Medal in 1952.

- There is a branch of Madame Tussaud's Wax Museum in New York City. One of its exhibits is a wax figure of Whoopi Goldberg.

- Madame Tussaud created death masks from the severed heads of France's King Louis XVI and his queen, Marie Antoinette.

Suspect 4—Armand Bonhomie

- Birdsboro, Pennsylvania, is about 12 miles southeast of Wyomissing, Pennsylvania.

- *To Kill a Mockingbird* won the Pulitzer Prize for Fiction in 1961.

- *Sturm und drang* translates as "storm and stress" and means high emotionalism or turmoil.

- *Oiseau de raillerie* means "bird of mocking remarks."

- Gioachino Rossini wrote the opera *La Gazza Ladra* and the 1829 opera *Guillaume Tell (William Tell)*.

- *La Gazza Ladra,* which is Italian for "the thieving magpie," is based on the true story of a French servant girl who was executed for a theft that was actually perpetrated by a magpie. In Rossini's opera the girl is rescued at the last minute.

- Giovanni Gherardini was a Milanese doctor and poet who wrote the words for *La Gazza Ladra.*

The Mystery of the Duplicitous Document

The Crime

Even for Dusten, Dusten & Molden, the prestigious art and antiques auction house, the sale was an exciting event. Four documents relating to the early history of the United States were up for bid. The sale was about to begin when the scream of Dorian Dusten III's administrative assistant tore through the auction hall. She had found her employer dead at his desk.

He had been struck on the back of his head with a small marble bust of Benjamin Franklin. The computer file he had been working on at the time of his death had been deleted. Fortunately, he had been able to send one e-mail before he died. Sent to a close friend, Bernard Vieillard, it read, *"Un des documents en vente aujourd'hui est une contrefaçon. J'ai l'intention d'appeler la police."* The only other clue was a scrawled note beneath the body. It read "Julian—Gregorian."

The Question

Who killed Dorian Dusten III?

The Suspects

Suspect 1—Frederick Steuben

Frederick Steuben, dealer in historical documents, claims to have been born in Washington, Connecticut, which is about two miles northwest of Horse Heaven, 200 years after Paul Revere's ride.

"I specialize in documents that reveal the personalities behind historical events," Frederick Steuben explained. "Consider the British surrender at Yorktown. The British general Charles Lord Cornwallis was galled beyond measure that the country with the greatest military might in the world had been defeated by what he considered to be a band of upstart, untrained rebels. He couldn't bring himself to surrender his sword to General Washington, so he sent this note to his own second-in-command, Charles O'Hara: "Take my sword to Comte de Rochambeau. I have no stomach to surrender to that jay-bird leader of the peasant traitors who calls himself **General** Washington. Tell Rochambeau *'Sans aide des officiers français il n'y aurait pas une victoire coloniale aujourd'hui.'*"

"Well, Rochambeau wasn't going to allow that! He sent O'Hara to General Washington. But even that was an insult. George Washington wasn't going to accept the sword of surrender from Cornwallis's second-in-command, so he sent **his** second-in-command, Major General Lincoln, to accept the sword of surrender from O'Hara. The surrender at Yorktown was a minuet of egos." Frederick Steuben chuckled. "History is full of stories like that. That's why I love it."

Frederick Steuben's Alibi: "I'm afraid I missed all of the excitement. I was in the men's room reading *Lies My Teacher Told Me: Everything Your American History Textbook Got Wrong* by James Loewen," he explained, pulling a well-worn paperback book out of his jacket pocket. "I was in a stall. I don't believe anyone else saw me."

Suspect 2—Julian du Motier

Julian du Motier, dealer in historical documents, claims to have been born in Washington, Utah, which is in Washington County, 200 years after George III became King of England.

"With a name like du Motier how could I not be fascinated by the *histoire de* Lafayette? I'm referring, of course, to Marie Joseph Paul Yves Roch Gilbert du Motier, the Marquis de Lafayette. He was just shy of his twentieth birthday when he joined the Continental Army as a major general, but he was a great soldier and a great friend of freedom. The affection he felt for America and its first president are evident in this letter he wrote to George Washington in March of 1798. No! No! You must not touch it without gloves! I will read it to you."

"*'Mon ami,* my darkest days are over. I, along with my beloved wife Adrienne and my daughters Anastasie and Virginie, have been released from Olmutz Prison. Now that my son George Washington Lafayette has returned to Paris we are once more a family. My son speaks often of your generosity in opening Mount Vernon to him as a sanctuary in his flight. That all three of our children survived the Reign of Terror is a fact that in some measure has eased Adrienne's grief over the loss of her mother, grandmother and sister to the guillotine. I remain, now and through eternity, your truest friend and greatest admirer, as you shall always remain *mon deuxiéme pére.*' The letter is signed, simply, Gilbert," Julian du Motier said as he wiped a tear from the corner of his eye. "Theirs was one of the greatest friendships in American history."

Julian du Motier's Alibi: "I will tell you the truth, but please do not tell my wife. I was in the alley behind the auction house smoking a cigarette. I am ashamed of my weakness," Julian du Motier confessed. "Weakness is unbecoming to a du Motier."

Suspect 3—Martha Custis Dandridge

Martha Custis Dandridge, dealer in historical documents, claims to have been born in Washington, Michigan, which is approximately 40 miles southeast of Mount Vernon, Michigan, 200 years after Nathan Hale was executed by firing squad.

"When I was going over a box of documents I had bought at an estate sale I was immediately drawn to one small piece of paper with lovely, old-fashioned writing," Martha Dandridge told us. "When I realized who it was from I was absolutely thrilled. This is a thank-you note from George Washington's mother to a friend, with whom she and her family had spent the New Year's holiday. This is what it says."

"'March 1, 1732. Dear Antonia, Please forgive my tardiness in letting two months pass before thanking you for your more than gracious hospitality at the New Year holiday. As you know by

now, our precious child was born a little more than a week ago, on February 22. He is a comely child, in aspect much like his father. We have chosen to name him George and hope for great things, both for and from him. With great affection and gratitude for all your kindness, I remain your most loyal friend, Mary Ball Washington.'"

Martha Custis Dandridge's Alibi: "I was on my way to Dorian Dusten's office to withdraw the document from the sale because I knew the rumors about a forgery would decrease the bid prices. But I never got to his office. I met Virginia Gregorian in the hallway. She was very upset and I tried to calm her down. Then we heard Dorian Dusten's assistant scream. Thank God I didn't get to his office sooner. I might have surprised the killer and been a victim myself."

Suspect 4—Virginia Gregorian

Virginia Gregorian, dealer in historical documents, claims to have been born in Washington, Kansas, which is about 20 miles "as the crow flies" northeast of Strawberry, 200 years after the Boston Massacre.

"My specialty is music," Virginia Gregorian explained. "The document I was offering at the Dusten, Dusten & Molden sale was a piece of sheet music published in London in the latter part of the eighteenth century that reveals how the song 'Yankee Doodle Dandy' permuted through the years. It was originally sung by British officers to mock their colonial allies during the French and Indian War, and it was certainly used to ridicule the American colonists at the beginning of the Revolution. It was purportedly played by the British when their troops left Boston to reinforce British troops already fighting the colonists at Concord and Lexington. Tradition claims that the colonial soldiers began singing it, with their own verses added, of course, as they beat the British back from those battles. By the end of 1775, when the colonists had the British army confined to Boston, 'Yankee Doodle Dandy' had become the unofficial anthem of American troops, as you can clearly hear in this verse." Virginia Gregorian slipped on a pair of reading glasses and read from a page of sheet music carefully protected by a glassine sleeve. "'Sheep's Head and Vinegar / Buttermilk and Tansy / Boston Is a Yankee Town / Sing Hey Doodle Dandy.'"

Virginia Gregorian's Alibi: "I was very upset by the rumor that one of the documents on sale was a forgery. I considered withdrawing the 'Yankee Doodle Dandy' sheet music from the sale for fear the rumor would taint the credibility of my item, but I wanted Frederick Steuben's advice before I did anything rash. He's a very smart man. And adorable, don't you think?" Virginia Gregorian blushed like a schoolgirl. "But I couldn't find him, and I bumped into that boring Dandridge woman in the hallway. Then we heard the scream, and you know the rest."

The Solution

The reason Dorian Dusten III was killed lies in the e-mail he sent to Bernard Vieillard: *Un des documents en vente aujour-d'hui est une contrefaçon. J'ai l'intention d'appeler la police.* (One of the documents on sale today is a counterfeit. I intend to call the police.) The key to the counterfeit document lies in the note that was found underneath his body. "Julian—Gregorian" does not refer to two of the suspects. It refers to the differences between the Julian and Gregorian calendars.

When George Washington was born, the Julian calendar was in use in Britain and the colonies, and, according to that calendar, the date of Washington's birth was February 11, 1731. In 1752, Britain and its colonies adopted the Gregorian calendar because that calendar more adequately dealt with the problem of gaining days over the course of many years. The adoption of a new calendar meant that the British and the American colonists of 1752 had to make three changes:

- Eleven days were dropped from the calculation of time. (So February 11 became February 22.)

- The New Year, which had previously been celebrated on The Feast of Annunciation on March 25, was shifted to January 1.

- All changes were retroactive, which means the new calendar was also used to calculate dates that came before 1752. People like George Washington who were born between January 1 and March 25 in the years before 1752 found themselves with totally new birth dates, 11 days and—because of the change of date for New Year's—one year later than their original birth dates.

Although George Washington's birth date is often given as February 22, 1732 (Gregorian), his mother, writing a letter shortly after his birth, would have used the Julian date of February 11, 1731. She also would not have been thanking a friend for hospitality extended at a recent New Year holiday, since the New Year was yet to come on March 25. Martha Dandridge did not understand that when she forged Mary Ball Washington's thank-you note, but Dorian Dusten III knew exactly what the date discrepancies meant. When Martha Dandridge heard the rumor that a forgery was suspected, she knew she was about to be found out. When she ran into Virginia Gregorian in the hallway she was not on her way to Dorian Dusten III's office, as she had claimed. She was coming from his office after she had killed him with a conveniently placed marble bust of Benjamin Franklin and had deleted the file of evidence from his computer.

Information About the Suspects

Suspect 1—Frederick Steuben

- Washington, Connecticut, is about two miles northwest of Horse Heaven, Connecticut.

- Paul Revere rode to warn the colonists of an impending British attack on April 18, 1775. Frederick Steuben was born 200 years later, in 1975.

- *Sans aide des officiers français il n'y aurait pas une victoire coloniale aujour-d'hui* means "without the help of French officers there would not be a colonial victory today."

- When Charles Lord Cornwallis surrendered at Yorktown, Virginia, he sent his second-in-command, Charles O'Hara, to deliver his sword to Comte de Rochambeau, who sent O'Hara to General Washington. George Washington had his second-in-command, Major General Benjamin Lincoln, accept the sword.

- *Lies My Teacher Told Me: Everything Your American History Textbook Got Wrong* was written by James Loewen.

Suspect 2—*Julian du Motier*

- Washington, Utah, is in Washington County, Utah.

- George III became King of England in 1760. Julian du Motier was born 200 years later, in 1960.

- Marie Joseph Paul Yves Roch Gilbert du Motier, the Marquis de Lafayette, was born on September 6, 1757, so he was just shy of his twentieth birthday when he joined the Continental Army as a major general on July 31, 1777.

- *Mon ami* means "my friend."

- Lafayette, his wife, Adrienne, and their daughters, Anastasie and Virginie, spent two years in Olmutz Prison.

- George Washington Lafayette was sent to the United States, where he was a guest of George Washington at Mount Vernon.

- Adrienne du Motier's mother, grand-mother and sister all went to the guillotine during the Reign of Terror.

- *Mon deuxiéme pére* means "my second father."

Suspect 3—*Martha Custis Dandridge*

- Washington, Michigan, is southeast of Mount Vernon, Michigan, but it is four miles, not 40 miles, away.

- Nathan Hale was executed by the British in 1776, but he died by hanging, not by firing squad. Martha Custis Dandridge was born 200 years later, in 1976.

- Mary Ball Washington was George Washington's mother.

- Mary Ball Washington, writing shortly after the birth of her son, George, would have used the Julian calendar, not the Gregorian calendar. The Gregorian calendar was not adopted by the colonists until 1752. By the Julian calendar, George Washington's birth would have occurred on February 11, 1731, and the New Year holiday would have been celebrated on March 25.

Suspect 4—*Virginia Gregorian*

- Washington, Kansas, is northeast of Strawberry, Kansas, about 20 miles away "as the crow flies."

- The Boston Massacre occurred in March of 1770. Virginia Gregorian was born in 1970.

- "Yankee Doodle Dandy" was originally sung by British officers to mock their colonial allies during the French and Indian War. It was purportedly played by the British when their troops left Boston to reinforce British troops already fighting the colonists at Concord and Lexington. Tradition claims that the colonial soldiers began singing it, with their own verses added, as they beat the British back from those battles. By the end of 1775, when the colonists had the British army confined to Boston, "Yankee Doodle Dandy" had become the unofficial anthem of American troops.

• Sheet music published in London in the late eighteenth century contained this verse: "Sheep's Head and Vinegar / Buttermilk and Tansy / Boston Is a Yankee Town / Sing Hey Doodle Dandy."

The Mystery of the Murdered Millionaire

The Crime

Clarence Moneybucks, the 98-year-old founder of the Moneybucks chain of department stores, had suffered a stroke, two heart attacks, diabetes, prostate cancer, chronic obstructive pulmonary disease, psoriasis and Guillain-Barre Syndrome, so it came as no surprise when his wife found him dead in his bed at 8 a.m. The cause of death, however, did come as a surprise. An autopsy revealed that Clarence Moneybucks had died of *Clostridium botulinum* neurotoxin poisoning. No one else in the Moneybucks household reported symptoms of a food-borne illness. In fact, there were no other reports of food-borne illness in the entire county in the two weeks prior to or following Clarence Moneybucks's death.

The Question

Who is responsible for Clarence Moneybucks's death?

The Suspects

Suspect 1—Mercy LaRue Moneybucks

Mercy LaRue Moneybucks, Clarence Moneybucks's wife, claims to have been born in Cheesequake, New Jersey, which is about eight miles northeast of Spotswood, the year that *Rabbit Is Rich* by John Updike won the Pulitzer Prize for Fiction.

"I met Clarence over the phone a year ago," the very lovely Mercy LaRue Moneybucks told us in a breathy whisper. "I was working as a telemarketer for a line of kitchenware products, and we started talking about other things, like what I wanted to do with my life. He invited me to his house for dinner, and I never left. I started taking care of Clarence, then we got married."

"I always wanted to be a nurse. Like her." Mercy LaRue Moneybucks gestured to a biography of Florence Nightingale that was lying on a nearby table. "But Clarence told me I am not like Florence Nightingale at all. I am more like Mary Seacole. He said Seacole came from a poor background like mine, not a middle-class British family like Nightingale's. And Seacole faced racial prejudice. But she did what she wanted to do no matter how many obstacles she had to face. Almost the last thing Clarence said to me was, 'Honey, people aren't going to believe that a woman who looks like you is smart. You go prove them wrong.' That's why I loved him. I don't care if he leaves me any money in his will. He's already given me more than I could ever repay."

Mercy LaRue Moneybucks's Alibi: "I looked in on Clarence just before I went to bed at 11 o'clock. He seemed unable to focus his eyes when he looked at me, but I just thought he was tired. I had no idea he was dying." A tear trailed down her cheek. "I didn't even kiss him good night."

Suspect 2—Buck Morov

Buck Morov, Mercy LaRue Moneybucks's cousin, claims to have been born in Hamburg, New Jersey, which is "just a mile or two from the deep-woods wilderness area of Mount Pisgah," 220 years after Eugene Aram died of food poisoning.

"Yeah, I've been staying here for about two months now while I get on my feet. Mercy is family, you know. Family takes care of family. Anyway, I got a job over at Lake Front College, doing maintenance and cleanup in the Home Economics Lab. They do a lot of work with home canning safety. Hey, at least there is always food lying around." Buck Morov grinned. "Half of the lab is set aside for foods that don't need that much processing because they have really low pH levels. Stuff like asparagus, beans, squash, corn, carrots, you know, food that's high in acid content. And the other half of the lab, what I call 'skull and crossbones land,' is the really dangerous low-acid, high pH stuff, like peaches, pears, tomatoes and sauerkraut. Hey, all you need to do is smell sauerkraut to know that stuff can be lethal."

"But I quit a few days ago," Buck admitted, "when they asked me to dispose of a bunch of stool samples from laboratory animals that had died after eating improperly canned shrimp, and I realized that they weren't talking about furniture.

So, I'm back looking for work again. Something more pleasant this time."

Buck Morov's Alibi: "I hardly ever saw the old coot because Mercy didn't want me to bother him, but I did see him briefly the day before he died. I was walking down the hallway, and that weird lawyer of his poked his head out of the bedroom and said, 'You! Come witness a document.' So, I went in and signed what Moore shoved in front of me and then I left. No, I didn't read what I signed. The lawyer gave me the creeps, and the old guy was just revolting, the way he'd dropped egg salad all over his bed."

Suspect 3—Dorchen Muenchkin

Dorchen Muenchkin, Clarence Moneybucks's cook and housekeeper, claims to have been born in Bad Homburg Vor Der Hohe, the famous spa and resort town in central Germany, the year that James Stewart starred in the movie *Anatomy of a Murder.*

"I cannot believe that the old gentleman is gone!" Dorchen Muenchkin pressed a handkerchief to her tear-swollen eyes. "Mr. Clarence was like that Russian monk Rasputin. First his enemies poisoned him, then they shot him, then they beat him, then they tied him up and threw him through a hole in the ice into a cold river. He died, of course, but who expected it after everything else he'd lived through? Mr. Clarence lived through everything else that happened to him, including **that woman,** who was far too young to love someone his age, but would the old fool listen?"

"Ich vergiftete den alten mann!" Dorchen Muenchkin let out a sudden, keening

wail. "But it wasn't my fault! That woman had me running here, running there, doing this, doing that ... 'Dorchen, go into town and get some Brewer's yeast. Dorchen, please cut back on the salt in Mr. Moneybucks's meals. Dorchen, you're going to have to keep the house free of dust ...' Who did she think she was to come in here and issue orders like that?" Dorchen Muenchkin asked bitterly. "With all of her incessant demands, I didn't have time to cook decent meals for the gentleman anymore, so I cut a few corners. My boyfriend, George, works in the cafeteria at Lake Front College and he started bringing me food at the end of the lunch shift. Mr. Clarence loved their egg salad. He had it for a late lunch the last day of his life."

Dorchen Muenchkin's Alibi: "Alibi? Why are you asking me stupid questions about an alibi? I've already confessed. But the real culprit is that gold digger who bewitched him."

Suspect 4—Les S. Moore

Les S. Moore, Clarence Moneybucks's lawyer, claims to have been born in Sandwich, New Hampshire, "which is east of West Sandwich and west of East Sandwich and north of South Sandwich, but not south of North Sandwich because there is no North Sandwich," 275 years after Jean Baptiste Lully died of food poisoning.

"I've already offered to serve as Ms. Muenchkin's legal counsel," Les S. Moore informed us. "*Ex gratia,* of course, as a *quid pro quo* for all the coffee and muffins I've had in her kitchen over the years I've been Clarence Moneybucks's legal adviser. She is clearly *in delicto* the perpetrator of an *actus reus,* but I think the jury will be lenient when they fully understand that the *res gestae* in this case sprang from Ms. Muenchkin's reaction to the household's descent into a condition *contra bonos mores* and her perhaps overly naive desire to remain her employer's *custos morum."*

"Well, I'm sorry you're not well enough educated to understand what I've been saying." Les. S. Moore reacted irritably to our request that he speak in simple English sentences. "I was with Clarence Moneybucks in the late afternoon. I brought him some papers to sign. He was changing his will to exclude Mercy." He lowered his voice to a conspiratorial whisper. "He finally understood that she had

married him for his money and was carrying on in his own house with that so-called cousin of hers. He didn't leave her entirely destitute," Les S. Moore added. "He wasn't an unkind or unfair man. He left her $50,000, the same amount, he pointed out, that Marilyn Monroe left her two former husbands, Joe DiMaggio and Arthur Miller, in her last will and testament. But the bulk of his estate was to go to a charitable fund that I would administer at my discretion."

Les S. Moore's Alibi: "I had nothing to do with Mr. Moneybucks's unfortunate demise. *Cadit quaestio."*

The Solution

Clarence Moneybucks's inability to focus his eyes when Mercy said goodnight to him at 11 p.m. was probably an early symptom of the *Clostridium botulinum* poisoning that would end his life by morning. The onset of *Clostridium botulinum* symptoms usually occurs 12 to 36 hours after ingestion, though onset can occur as early as four hours after ingestion, especially in someone as frail as Clarence Moneybucks. The egg salad he had for a late lunch the day before he died is the most likely source of the neurotoxin that killed him.

Egg salad is the culprit in a good many food-borne illness outbreaks, but the guilty bacteria are usually *Salmonella*, *Staphlococcus*, *Campylobacter*, *Shigella* or *Clostridium perfringens* (which is known, for good reason, as "the cafeteria germ"), not the *Clostridium botulinum* that caused Clarence Moneybucks's death. In addition, there were no other cases of botulism reported in the area. Only Clarence Moneybucks ingested the botulism neurotoxin. It is remotely possible, but highly unlikely, that the egg salad, in the condition it was served at Lake Front College's cafeteria, caused Clarence Moneybucks's death but no other illness. It is far more likely that something tainted the egg salad after it left the cafeteria.

It is also very suspicious that Clarence Moneybucks's will was changed less than 24 hours before his death. The most likely scenario is that Mercy's cousin and Clarence Moneybucks's lawyer worked together to trick the elderly gentleman into signing a new will, then poisoned him before Clarence Moneybucks or Mercy could discover what they'd done. Through his job in Lake Front College's Home Economics Lab, Buck Morov had access to improperly canned shrimp and other foods that might contain the *Clostridium botulinum* neurotoxin. Les S. Moore would have been able to introduce a bit of that material into Clarence's egg salad while he visited him the afternoon before his death. The motive, of course, was greed. Les. S. Moore would be the administrator of the Moneybucks fortune, with sole discretion about how the funds would be dispersed. He probably promised Buck Morov a percentage. Apparently, Buck was not as loyal to the idea of family as Mercy was.

Information About the Suspects

Suspect 1—Mercy LaRue Moneybucks

- According to Mapquest's mileage key, Cheesequake, New Jersey, is about eight miles northeast of Spotswood, New Jersey.

- *Rabbit Is Rich* by John Updike won the Pulitzer Prize for Fiction in 1982.

- Florence Nightingale came from a middle-class British family.

- Mary Seacole was a Jamaican woman from a poor background who faced racial discrimination. When her request to be sent to the Crimea as a nurse was denied, she went anyway.

Suspect 2—Buck Morov

- According to Mapquest's driving directions, Hamburg, New Jersey, is about 14 miles east of Mount Pisgah, New Jersey.

- Mount Pisgah, New Jersey, is a state park, not a deep-woods wilderness area.

- Eugene Aram was hanged as a murderer in 1759. Buck Morov was born 220 years later, in 1979.

- Asparagus, beans, squash, corn and carrots are high pH, low-acid foods. They are at risk for the development of *Clostridium botulinum* and require more care when canning.

- Peaches, pears, tomatoes and sauerkraut are low pH, high-acid foods, which require less care in home canning.

- *Clostridium botulinum* produces a neurotoxin. It would grow on improperly canned shrimp.

Suspect 3—Dorchen Muenchkin

- Bad Homburg Vor Der Hohe is a famous spa and resort town in central Germany.

- James Stewart starred in the movie *Anatomy of a Murder* in 1959.

- Rasputin, a Russian monk and adviser to the royal Romanov family, was hard to kill. His enemies poisoned him, then shot him, beat him and finally tied him up and threw him through a hole in the ice into the River Neva.

- *Ich vergiftete den alten mann!* means "I poisoned the old man."

Suspect 4—Les S. Moore

- Not only is there a Sandwich, Sandwich Landing and East Sandwich in New Hampshire, there is also a North Sandwich.

- Jean Baptise Lully died in 1687, but he died of gangrene—or, in some accounts, blood poisoning—not of food poisoning. Les S. Moore was born 275 years later, in 1962.

- *Ex gratia* means "out of kindness" or "voluntary."

- *Quid pro quo* means "something for something."

- *In delicto* means "at fault."

- *Actus reus* means "a guilty deed."

- *Res gestae* means "the thing done."

- *Contra bonos mores* means "contrary to good morals."

- *Custos morum* means "guardian of morals."

- *Cadit quaestio* means "the matter admits to no further argument."

- Joe DiMaggio and Arthur Miller were former husbands of Marilyn Monroe, but she left nothing to them in her will. Marilyn Monroe's beneficiaries included her personal secretary, May Reis; her mother, Gladys Baker; her half-sister, Berniece Miracle; Patricia Rosten and her parents; Mrs. Michael Chekhov; Lee Strasberg; and psychiatrist Marianne Kris.

Additional Information

- *Clostridium botulinum* contamination occurs primarily in improperly canned low-acid foods and meats.

- Symptoms of *Clostridium botulinum* poisoning include blurred and double vision, slurred speech, dry mouth, difficulty swallowing, paralysis that descends through the body and paralysis of the breathing muscles. Symptoms generally appear 12 to 36 hours after ingestion of the contaminated food, but symptoms can appear as soon as four hours or as long as eight days following ingestion. Effects of *Clostridium botulinum* are even more severe in people who are very young, elderly or in poor health.

The Mystery of the Murderous Mushrooms

The Crime

Olive Pitt, the caustic insult-comedian whom *People* magazine voted Funniest Woman in America two years in a row, is dead. Following an autopsy, the medical examiner ruled that the cause of death was liver failure secondary to ingestion of 80 milligrams of *Amanita phalloides*. A reconstruction of Olive Pitt's last week of life revealed the following timeline:

Monday, September 8, 11 a.m.: Olive Pitt and her husband, Brad Ladd, were guests on *Edible Delights*, a television cooking show presided over by chef Pierre Potage. Potage displayed a variety of mushrooms, both edible and inedible, and used the edible mushrooms in an omelet. Olive Pitt ate the entire omelet, while her husband nibbled on the parsley.

Monday, September 8, noon: Olive Pitt and her husband left the set of *Edible Delights*. Brad Ladd said they drove directly to their isolated mountain cabin so Olive could get some much-needed rest and privacy.

Tuesday, September 9, 9:30 p.m.: Olive Pitt spoke by phone to her agent. She said that she had suffered a bout of flu the night before, with vomiting, diarrhea, stomach pain and headache, but said that she was feeling much better now. She told her agent that she planned to stay at her cabin another week and promised to call when she arrived back in Los Angeles.

Wednesday, September 10, 8 a.m.: Brad Ladd arrived at the Los Angeles airport and booked a flight to Trenton, New Jersey. He arrived in Trenton at 5 p.m. Eastern Standard Time. He spent the following week visiting his sister.

Thursday, September 18, 3:30 p.m.: Brad Ladd returned to the mountain cabin and found his wife dead in her bed. He immediately called the police. The medical examiner estimated that Olive Pitt had been dead about two days. Although she must have been in gastrointestinal distress, Olive Pitt did not use the portable phone beside her bed to call for help.

The Question

What—or who—killed Olive Pitt?

The Suspects

Suspect 1—Pierre Potage

Pierre Potage, television chef, claims to have been born in Coat-Meal, France, which is west of Plabennec in the area of France known as Brittany, the year that Emeril Lagasse was born in New Bedford, Massachusetts.

"I did not serve Olive Pitt a tainted omelet! *C'est impossible!*" Pierre Potage insisted. "I admit that I was not at my best during the taping of the show. Madame Pitt and I had had a rather unpleasant exchange. She was insulted that I planned to cook a mere omelet for a star of her magnitude. She said that when she visited the set of Julia Child's cooking show, Julia served her an entire chicken larded with bacon. 'Faw,' I said. 'I am tired to death of hearing about Julia, Julia, Julia, Julia! Always with the sauces and the butter and the bacon fat. *Les femmes ruinent toujours les bonnes aliments.* This woman was not a chef. She was a government operative! Oh, yes! When people say she worked for the CIA, they do not mean the famous cooking school, Culinary Institute of the Americas, they mean the Central Intelligence Agency. She should have remained a spy and left the world of cuisine to those who know what they are doing!"

"It was a rash thing for me to say," Pierre Potage admitted. "Madame Pitt howled with laughter, just like a *babouin,* as we would say in my language. Then she said she planned to repeat my remarks to *People* magazine the next time she was interviewed. I saw then how unfortunate my loss of temper could be for me."

Pierre Potage's Alibi: "It is true that I was upset. I may have been distracted. But I used only the mushrooms from the basket of edible mushrooms. I am positive."

Suspect 2—Babs Bacon

Babs Bacon, assistant to chef Potage, claims to have been born in Spanish Fork, Utah, which is east of Utah Lake.

"My real name is Babette," Babs informed us. "Like the title character in the movie that won the Academy Award for Best Foreign Film when I was four years old. I don't know anything about food," she confessed. "I just try to do my job, which isn't always easy around here. The day you're asking about, chef Potage was in a nasty mood, Chili was upset about the mushrooms and Olive Pitt was so clumsy she knocked the labels off the baskets of mushrooms when she walked by them. I put the labels back on. Do you think I could have put them on the wrong baskets?" Her eyes widened with horror. "Oh, my heavens, do you think I killed Olive Pitt?"

"Let me think." She placed a trembling hand against her suddenly pale cheek. "The label that said *Amanita muscaria et phalloides. N'employez pas ces champignons—* I put that one on the basket of red mushrooms. I'm sure of it. All of the mushrooms in that basket were red, flecked with white, like the kind of mushrooms you'd see in a book of fairy tales. I remember Mr. Pitt said they were called Fly Agarics and that when he was a child his family used to crush them in milk and sugar to make a poisoned bait for flies. Mr. Pitt was really nice about helping me. And handsome." Babs flushed. "He was so much nicer than his wife."

Babette Bacon's Alibi: "I don't really have an alibi, do I?"

Suspect 3—Chili Carney

Chili Carney, camera operator, claims to have been born in Tabasco, which is in the Mexican state of Zacatecas, not in the Mexican state of Tabasco, the year that Mitsugoro Bando VIII died from eating fugu.

"I could not believe my eyes," Chili Carney told us. "Potage had a basket of Fly Agarics and Death Caps on the counter. He should not have had anything that poisonous anywhere near his food preparation area. It reminded me of the day he cooked fugu. One *Diodon holacanthus* contains enough tetrodotoxin to kill 30 people. It is 1,200 times more toxic than cyanide. I prepared a report on the risks of eating fugu and gave it to the producer. Do you know what he told me? He said that Potage didn't like my negative attitude and that if I couldn't learn how to be a team player I would have to find work somewhere else, maybe making infomercials. So I said, 'Fine. Let Potage kill someone with his flamboyant, high-risk foods. Maybe then you'll take my warnings seriously.'"

Chili Carney's Alibi: "I was doing my best to film every move Potage made. It's obvious that one of the poisonous mushrooms ended up in the omelet he served to Olive Pitt. Unfortunately, I wasn't able to capture his mistake on tape."

Suspect 4—Brad Ladd

Brad Ladd, Olive Pitt's husband, was born in Mushroom Farms, Pennsylvania, which, he claims, is "very close to the Pocono Playhouse, where I got my early theatrical experience, and on the edge of the Allegheny National Forest, where I learned to love nature." He claims to have been born 75 years after Fannie McDonald Farmer's *New England Cooking School Cookbook* was first published.

"Olive was a magnificent comedian," Brad Ladd informed us as he wiped a tear from his cheek. "Very physical, very good at pratfalls and double-takes, just like her idol, Carole Lombard. And now she's gone at a young age, just like Lombard. I remember Carole Lombard's funeral. I was just a child then, of course, but I remember the enormous crowd that gathered for one last sight of her and how her husband bore his sorrow with quiet dignity. I must remember that now. I'm thinking of having her buried near the Garden of Serenity in Westwood Memorial Park so she can be with her idol through all eternity."

Brad Ladd's Alibi: "I wasn't with her when she died. I wasn't even in the state. We ..." A sob caught in his throat. "We had a fight. Over another woman. Olive was very jealous. I had had a flirtation. Perhaps a bit more than a flirtation," he admitted. "Olive found a letter the young woman had written to me. She became enraged and told me to get out. So I left. I drove to the Los Angeles airport and took a plane to New Jersey to visit my sister. I knew Olive would calm down eventually. She always did. So I waited a week, then I flew back to California and drove to the cabin. But by the time I got there Olive was already gone. How can I ever forgive myself?" he cried. "My darling Olive died without me."

The Solution

Pierre Potage cooked the omelet that killed Olive Pitt, but the real murderer was Olive's husband, Brad. He knew enough about poisonous mushrooms to recognize the Death Cap mushroom in the basket of Fly Agarics. While he was assisting—and no doubt flirting with—Babs, he slipped the Death Cap out of the basket of inedible mushrooms and placed it in the basket of edible mushrooms. (The label said *Amanita muscaria et phalloides,* but Babs said all of the mushrooms in the basket of inedible fungi were red. The *Amanita phalloides* is not red, so it must have been removed from the inedible basket.) Chef Potage might have recognized the Death Cap as poisonous—though many people don't—but he was angry and distracted. He chopped up the mushroom, incorporated it into an omelet and served it to his guests. Brad Ladd did not partake, so his wife ate the entire omelet, guaranteeing that she would ingest more than enough amatoxin to cause death.

The first symptoms of *Amanita phalloides* poisoning occurred about 12 hours after Olive ate the omelet. The fact that she felt better the next day led Olive to believe that the vomiting, diarrhea and headaches were caused by a bout of flu. But Brad knew that a period of improvement is often part of the progression of Death Cap poisoning, and he knew what to expect. He made sure his wife found the letter from another woman so he would have an excuse to leave. He hid her cell phone so she couldn't call for help, then he left her alone in their isolated mountain cabin to die. He estimated it would take anywhere from 4 to 10 more days for the toxin to prove fatal.

Information About the Suspects

Suspect 1—Pierre Potage

- Coat-Meal, France, is west of Plabennec in the area of France known as Brittany.

- Emeril Lagasse was born in 1959 in Fall River, not New Bedford, Massachusetts.

- *Les femmes ruinent toujours les bonnes aliments* means "women always ruin good food."

- Julia Child worked for the Office of Strategic Services—a government intelligence agency that was the precursor of the Central Intelligence Agency—in Ceylon and China.

- The famous cooking school known as the CIA is The Culinary Institute of America, not Culinary Institute of the Americas.

- *Babouin* means "baboon."

Suspect 2—Babs Bacon

- Spanish Fork, Utah, is east of Utah Lake.

- *Babette's Feast* won the Academy Award for Best Foreign Film in 1987. If Babs was four years old at the time, she was born in 1983.

- The *Amanita muscaria,* also known as the Fly Agaric, is a red mushroom with white flecks. Crushed in milk and sugar, it makes an effective poisoned bait for flies.

- The *Amanita phalloides* is the Death Cap mushroom. It is not red.

Suspect 3—Chili Carney

- Tabasco, Mexico, is in the Mexican state of Zacatecas, not the Mexican state of Tabasco.

- Mitsugoro Bando VIII died from eating fugu in 1975.

- Fugu, also known as the *Diodon holacanthus* or blowfish, is dangerous to eat because its liver contains enough tetrodotoxin to kill 30 people. Tetrodotoxin is 1,200 times more toxic than cyanide.

Suspect 4—Brad Ladd

- Mushroom Farms, Pennsylvania, is very close to the Pocono Playhouse, but it is not on the edge of the Allegheny National Forest.

- Fannie Farmer's middle name was Merritt, not McDonald.

- The name of Fannie Farmer's book was *Boston Cooking-School Cookbook,* not *New England Cooking School Cookbook.* It was first published in 1896. Brad Ladd was born 75 years later, in 1971.

- Carole Lombard's husband, Clark Gable, followed her instructions that no one except immediate family members and funeral home staff were to view her body after death. Even if she had not left those instructions, the state of her body after the plane crash in which she died would have precluded public viewing of her body. Her funeral was private. Carole Lombard is buried at Forest Lawn Memorial Park in Glendale, California, not in Westwood Memorial Park.

Additional Information

- The *Amanita phalloides* mushroom, also known as the Death Cap, is estimated to be the cause of 90 percent of all deaths by mushroom ingestion. An average-size Death Cap contains 30 to 90 milligrams of amatoxin. Five to 10 milligrams of amatoxin can cause death.

- The first symptoms of amatoxin poisoning can occur from 5 to 24 hours after ingestion, with the average onset in 12 hours. Symptoms—nausea, vomiting, diarrhea, abdominal pain and headaches—mimic symptoms of the flu. The first reaction is followed by a short phase of seeming improvement. Then the toxins destroy liver cells, causing liver and renal failure. Death can occur 2 to 10 days after ingestion of the Death Cap.

The Mystery of the Vanishing Vault Markers

The Crime

An alert fan noticed it on the World Wide Web—a complete set of vault markers for the Three Stooges offered to the highest bidder. "Six bronze plaques in a variety of styles." The fan pointed to the pictures on his computer screen as he read. "'Guaranteed originals.' What I want to know is, Where did they come from? Did someone pry the vault markers off their crypts? What kind of people would do that?" he demanded.

The Web page offered few clues. It was slick and attractive, with photos of the six Stooges and their corresponding vault markers. The only identification was an e-mail address, starghoul@abc.com, to which bids could be sent. However, the Web page is linked to a Web site for Morticia's Mortuary Musings, hosted by Silvia Sepulcro, an antiques dealer in Los Angeles, California. Sepulcro's Web site features dozens of photos of sculptures in various cemeteries around the country. "Nothing is beyond the reach of those who are willing to pay for what they desire," scrolls in red gothic lettering across the bottom of the screen.

The Question

Who is offering to sell a complete set of vault plaques from the graves of the Three Stooges?

The Suspects

Suspect 1—Silvia Sepulcro

Silvia Sepulcro, antiques dealer, claims to have been born in Port Arthur, Texas, "not far from the cemetery where Janis Joplin is buried," 75 years after Pauline Cushman was hanged as a spy.

"You want to know what 'Nothing is beyond the reach of those who are willing to pay for what they desire' means?" Silvia Sepulcro looked wearily amused. "It's a meaningless enticement. You don't believe everything you read on the Web, do you?"

"I sell antiques and antique reproductions. But mostly, I sell gossamer dreams of glory to lighten the banality of mundane, mediocre lives. People have always wanted to feel close to their gods, and movie stars are the only gods and goddesses we have left. People are willing to pay to touch what their idols have once touched. They're even willing to be crass and vulgar. Do you remember Lilyan Tashman's funeral? When she was buried in Santa Monica back in 1952, a crowd of fans surged forward with so much zeal they actually broke nearby grave markers and knocked Lilyan's grieving husband, Eddie Cantor, into the open grave. They were after flowers," Silvia Sepulcro added. "For a tawdry little souvenir of their favorite chanteuse they were willing to cast off all vestiges of civilized behavior. Those are the people I sell to, darling. I hold my nose and count my money. It's not a noble course of action, but it's not illegal, either."

Silvia Sepulcro's Alibi: "I have no idea who starghoul@abc.com is. I was contacted about putting the link on my Web site, and I did so because it is to my advantage to have a Web site with a multitude of interesting links. I also have a link to www.finda grave.com, but I don't guarantee the bodies will be where they say they are."

Suspect 2—Greg Graves

Greg Graves, originally Peter Graves, handyman and would-be actor, claims to have been born in Chicago, Illinois, "not far from the cemetery where Jim Henson is buried," 125 years after the death of Robert James Graves, the doctor who gave his name to Graves' Disease, a rare liver disorder.

"I'm out here trying to break into the movies," Greg Graves informed us. "Which ain't all that easy, you know? First of all, I had to change my name from Peter to Greg 'cause some old guy actor already had the name Peter Graves. The weird thing is, though, his original name was Arnett, so if he had stuck with his perfectly good name I could have stuck with mine. Everybody's better with his own name, know what I mean? Unless your name is something like Herkimer. That would be pretty bad for a movie star, I guess, though it's hard to call, what with some of the weird names floating around the business these days."

"What do I do for Silvia?" Greg Graves seemed surprised to have his rambling monologue interrupted by a direct question. "Oh, this, that and the other, if you know what I mean. I run a lot of stuff over from Konrad's place. Silvia sells it in her shop. People pay big money for funeral monuments, especially used monuments, if you can believe that. You know, I come from a family with a pretty spectacular monument. Honest! Dexter Graves. He's buried in Graceland Cemetery, you know, just like Elvis, and he's got this enormous statue by Auguste Rodin called *Pondering Eternity*. I've contacted the family about maybe selling it through Silvia, but they don't answer my letters. I'm like a distant cousin. But they could at least answer my letters, you know?"

Greg Graves's Alibi: "What is it I'm supposed to have done?"

Suspect 3—Tederic Tombe

Tederic Tombe, security guard at Forest Lawn Memorial Park (Glendale), claims to have been born in Paris, France, "not far from the cemetery where rock star Jim Morrison was buried." He says his birth came 50 years after George Edward Stanhope Molyneux Herbert, the fifth Earl of Carnarvon, died from what some people believe was a mummy's curse.

"I've been a guard here for the past six months," Tederic Tombe told us as he led us through the Freedom Mausoleum to the Sanctuary of Liberation. "Larry Fine is in here. Moe is over at Hillside Memorial Park in Culver City. Curly and Shemp are in the Home of Peace Memorial Park in East L.A. I was a guard over there for quite a few years before I got fired. I hit a rough patch, did a little too much drinking," Tederic Tombe admitted. "I've got a handle on the problem now. Anyhow, I've always thought it was a shame that the three Horwitz brothers aren't together, but the next of kin must have had their reasons. How many Stooges was that? Larry, Moe, Curly, Shemp ..." He counted on his fin-

gers. "Oh, yeah, Jerome Besser is here at Forest Lawn, and Curly-Joe DeRita is in Pierce Brothers Valhalla Memorial Park in North Hollywood."

"Ah, here's Larry." Tederic Tombe stopped in front of a vault with a marble face and simple inscription: Larry Fine 1902–1975. "It's here, isn't it?" Tederic Tombe voiced the obvious. "Maybe the cemetery discreetly replaced the vault face so no one would know that a theft like that could happen here. Or maybe there never was a theft. After all, *vous croyez ce que les voleurs vous disent?*

Tederic Tombe's Alibi: "I loved the Stooges! I wouldn't desecrate their graves like that!"

Suspect 4—Konrad Kirchhof

Konrad Kirchhof, owner of Kirchhof's Memorials, Inc., claims to have been born in Aberdeen, Washington, "not far from the cemetery where Kurt Cobain is buried," 100 years after Edmonia Lewis graduated from Oberlin College.

"Like it?" Konrad Kirchhof asked, gesturing to a large bronze grave marker that depicted winged angels leading children toward a setting sun. It's a copy of Hans Holbein's *Dance of Death*. "I think it's one of my best works. I do a lot of simpler pieces. Plaques, vault markers—Here Lies ... Dearly Beloved ... Blah, Blah, Blah. I did some work on Elvis Presley's grave when I was apprenticing at the Forest Hill Cemetery in Memphis, Tennessee. Ah, you should see that grave." Konrad Kirchhof brightened with the pleasure of memory. "Elvis is buried between his father, Vernon, and his Uncle Vester Presley inside a marble rotunda. There's an eternal flame in the middle of the rotunda, and all around the outside of the rotunda there are bronze reliefs of Elvis at different stages of his life. I assisted with the hound dog on the northeast corner. But people don't want that kind of stuff anymore," Konrad Kirchhof sighed. "They want tasteful markers. Name. Date. That's it. And they don't want to pay an arm and a leg for it, either. There's the irony. People pay big bucks to buy memorabilia of Hollywood stars, but not to honor their own loved ones."

Konrad Kirchhof's Alibi: "Why would I steal from the dead? I make my living honoring the dead."

The Solution

A crime is being committed, but it is not theft. It is fraud. Starghoul is offering six "guaranteed original" bronze vault plaques, but a search on the Find a Grave Web site reveals that the graves of the six men who portrayed the Three Stooges are marked by two bronze vault plaques (Shemp and Moe Howard), one marble vault face with a name and dates (Larry Fine), two in-ground grave markers (Curly-Joe DeRita and Joe Besser) and one large standing gravestone (Curly Howard).

Silvia Sepulcro, Greg Graves and Konrad Kirchhof are in the business of replicating and selling fake antique grave markers, monuments and mortuary art to gullible fans. Silvia is probably the brains of the business.

Information About the Suspects

Suspect 1—Silvia Sepulcro

- Janis Joplin's ashes were scattered over the Pacific Ocean.

- Pauline Cushman was sentenced to be hanged as a spy, but she was rescued when Union troops invaded Confederate headquarters in Shelbyville, Kentucky. She died in 1893 of an overdose of opium. Silvia Sepulcro was born 75 years later, in 1968.

- Lilyan Tashman was a minor actress, not a singer, whose 1934 funeral in Brooklyn, New York, brought out the worst in her fans. They did break nearby grave markers as they surged forward to grab flowers and funeral wreaths from the grave. Eddie Cantor was present at the funeral, but he was not knocked into the open grave.

Neither was Lilyan Tashman's husband, Edmund Lowe.

- The URL of Find a Grave is www.find agrave.com.

Suspect 2—Greg Graves

- Jim Henson was cremated, not buried.

- Robert James Graves, who died in 1853, gave his name to Graves Disease, but it is the most common disorder of the thyroid gland, not a rare disease of the liver. Greg Graves was born 125 years after the death of Robert James Graves, in 1978.

- Peter Graves's original name was Peter Aurness, not Arnett.

- Dexter Graves is buried in Graceland Cemetery, but it is in Chicago, not in Memphis, Tennessee, where Elvis Presley is buried.

- The statue on the Dexter Graves site, *Eternal Silence,* was sculpted by Lorado Taft.

Suspect 3—Tederic Tombe

- Jim Morrison is buried in Le Pere Lachaise Cemetery in Paris, France.

- George Edward Stanhope Molyneux Herbert, fifth Earl of Carnarvon, died shortly after the opening of King Tutankhamun's tomb, leading some people to conjecture that he was the victim of the mummy's curse. Other people believe he died from an infected mosquito bite.

- Larry Fine is interred at Freedom Mausoleum, Sanctuary of Liberation, at Forest Lawn Memorial Park (Glendale), California.

- Joe (Jerome) Besser is also interred at Forest Lawn Memorial Park (Glendale), California.

- Moe Howard is interred at Hillside Memorial Park in Culver City, California.

- Curly and Shemp Howard are interred at Home of Peace Cemetery in East Los Angeles, California.

- Curly-Joe DeRita is buried in Pierce Brothers Valhalla Memorial Park in North Hollywood, California.

- Larry Fine's vault has a marble face with the simple inscription "Larry Fine 1902–1975."

- Moe (Moses Horwitz), Curly (Jerome Lester Horwitz) and Shemp (Samuel Horwitz) were brothers. They all changed their last names to Howard.

- *Vous croyez ce que les voleurs vous disent?* means "You believe what robbers tell you?"

Suspect 4—Konrad Kirchhof

- Kurt Cobain's ashes were scattered in the Wishkah River in the state of Washington.

- Edmonia Lewis left Oberlin College in 1862, but she did not graduate. Konrad Kirchhof was born 100 years later, in 1962.

- Hans Holbein's *Dance of Death* depicts skeletons, not angels.

- Elvis Presley was originally interred in a crypt in the mausoleum at the Forest Hill Cemetery in Memphis, Tennessee, but his body was moved to his Graceland estate, where he now lies beside his father, Vernon, mother, Gladys, grandmother, Minnie Mae, and his brother, Jessie. Uncle Vester Presley was laid to rest at the Forest Hill Cemetery, Memphis, Tennessee.